Praise
Nana Camp

✯ ✯ ✯

I love that (the "open letter to my grandchildren"). I pray for our children and grandchildren. The enemy will attach in the dark. Our churches are empty. Pray for doctrine (to be taught).

Martin Mathis, retired financial controller of
Our Lady of the Lake University in San Antonio, Texas,
former partner with Deloitte and Touch,
grandfather of five, my brother

✯ ✯ ✯

This book is an inspiration, affirming and practical guide to grandmothers (and grandfathers) who wish to share with their grand children the joy and confidence that can come from a Christian lifestyle. Jaunts to take, activities to share, conversations to have—all are part of the process of enabling children to grow in faith. I wish every child could go to a Nana Camp!

Susan Santangelo, retired teacher and administrator,
University of Houston and
The Kinkaid School, Houston, Texas.
Grandmother of one

★ ★ ★

I had identical experiences with my cousins at Grandma's. I sense the emotion in your writing…wonderful. This is an inspiring book. I love the prayers and the idea of a mission statement. For so many who don't have memories of their grandparents or perhaps not good ones, you present a perspective of a loving grandparent/child relationship, that one can say, "oh, that's what it can look like." I enjoyed the literary journey and am excited to see what God will do with it. Wish you had written your book years ago. I have done a lot of creative fun things with grandchildren that they will remember, but just not worked in the spiritual as much as I could have. I know He is smiling.

Cathy Canfield Hicks, coordinator of
a Good News Club in Atlanta, Georgia,
grandmother of four

Marsha Eckermann has written a practical and inspiring biblical perspective of "redeeming the time with grandchildren"—whether they are yours or not. She challenges us early on to write our own personal "grandparent" mission statement with a particular focus on what we want our grandchildren to remember about us. Marsha "lets us in" on her secrets of adventure and imagination. She shows how to establish traditions and make them "platforms of opportunities" that teach a generation how to prepare the way for the next. Every grandmother/grandparent will enjoy and benefit from this delightful book.

Sue Sloan, first lady and wife of Dr. Robert Sloan,
president of Houston Baptist University, speaker,
grandmother of 20 +.

* * *

I want to send your letter to our grandchildren! Those thoughts are our thoughts exactly! It should be the thoughts of all grandparents!
Joan Owen,
mother of two
and grandmother of five

* * *

Every grandparent should be this proactive on the subject.
Dan Eckermann, retired president and CEO
of Latourneau Technologies, Inc,
author of *Notes on the Paths of Canon....with Impact on Christianity and Church*,
grandfather of two.

* * *

Your letter to your grandchildren is a wonderful epistle. My grand-nephews and grand-niece are growing up in a relatively benign environment, in the country, in the heart of Cajun-land and in the small town of Kaplan.... They are believers and conservative in their personal thinking. Yet, I am concerned about their progeny. I believe your letter may help.
Polly Hardee, Ph.D, Instructional Professor,
Economics Department, University of Houston

Nana Camp

XULON PRESS

A grandmother's story of bringing grandchildren to Jesus

Marsha Griffith Eckermann

Xulon Press
2301 Lucien Way #415
Maitland, FL 32751
407.339.4217
www.xulonpress.com

© 2021 by Marsha Griffith Eckermann

All rights reserved solely by the author. The author guarantees all contents are original and do not infringe upon the legal rights of any other person or work. No part of this book may be reproduced in any form without the permission of the author. The views expressed in this book are not necessarily those of the publisher.

Unless otherwise indicated, Scripture quotations taken from the New American Standard Bible (NASB). Copyright © 1960, 1962, 1963, 1968, 1971, 1972, 1973, 1975, 1977, 1995 by The Lockman Foundation. Used by permission. All rights reserved.

Printed in the United States of America

Paperback ISBN-13: 978-1-6628-1204-0
Hard Cover ISBN-13: 978-1-6628-1205-7
Ebook ISBN-13: 978-1-6628-1282-8

Dedicated to Hunter, Jackson, Joshua, Lily, Jacob, Joseph, Georgia, Genny

Without whom I would not
know this great adventure

★ ★ ★

To Lawrence (Poppy), who is my other bookend

Without whom I could not do what I do

★ ★ ★

And now unto Him Who is able to keep you from falling and to present you faultless before the presence of His glory with exceeding great joy; to the only Wise God, our Savior, through Jesus Christ our Lord, be all glory and majesty, dominion and authority, before all time and now and forever. Amen."

JUDE 24–25

Contents

Preface ix
Acknowledgements xiii

Introductions 3
Chapter 1   The Grandparent Bond (Odia) 5
Chapter 2   A Grandmother's Legacy: Building
Spiritual Family Relations 15
              Prayer 25
Chapter 3   Pass It On—a Command from Scripture 43
              Introduction (what is a legacy?) 43
              The Greatest Legacy Opportunity 50
              Why a legacy. 51
              Legacies from the Bible. 52
              Legacy of Prayer 58
              Legacy of the Word of God 60
              Legacy of Grace and Faith. 61
              The Power of a life's legacy. 68
              A Sober Warning 71
              When there is no legacy. 76
              Conclusion 77
Chapter 4   Let's go to Nana's House 81
              The home. 81

	Bedtime routine.	90
	Songs	94
	Simple Fun	97
	Holidays	100
	Travel	101
	No limits.	106
	Some fun things we have done.	108
	Every single time you are with them!!!!	109
Chapter 5	Nana Camp 101 (no parents, please)	111
	Themes of Nana Camp	120
	Texas	121
	Gone to Texas	123
	All About Animals	125
	The Lion of the Tribe of Judah	128
	More About Texas (2013)	132
	All About the Wind	135
	The Arts (2017)	138
	Girl time in Texas (2018)	140
	Sea Creatures (2019)	144
	The Moon, Sun, and Stars (2020)	146
Chapter 6	Find a sidekick, a Tonto, a "Memow"	153
Chapter 7	The Extended Blessings of Nana Camp	159
Chapter 8	Source of strength: Jesus	165
Chapter 9	One More Thing (in a nutshell)	171
Addendum #1	An Open Letter to My Grandchildren 2019	181
About the Author		187

Preface

★ ★ ★

Why in the world would I, Marsha Eckermann, write a book?

There are many wonderful volumes of literature. This is not one. There are many engaging novels. This is not one of those. There are many words of wisdom from which I have learned and profited in my personal walk. This, I hope, might be one of those.

My friend and mentor, Jeannette Clift George, wrote many powerful books in her lifetime. She wrote one entirely filled with insights into practical truth, and I loved it. She would say to us: *I dedicated that book to the Lord with great depth and commitment, trusting that it would reveal truth and change lives.... He gently said: Jeannette, I have already written that One.*

My inspiration as a grandmother comes from my own, Odia Ione McDavid Holtkamp. She was an amazing part of my life and my spiritual training. I hope you get to know her as you read my story.

Many friends have marveled at my appreciation for Grandma Odia and the ensuing story. Most do not have such an example. They wanted to hear more, and

I loved their encouragement. For them, I am delighted to share my story.

My journey as a grandmother began in 1998 and has since been filled with awesome responsibility and great fun. I have drawn from the fabric of Doctrine in my soul and my personal walk with Jesus Christ to guide me in this treasured role in life. As many other grandmothers began to ask what I did with my grandchildren I began to send them outlines of thoughts and plans for "Nana Camp." As my involvement in the lives of eight grandchildren grew and developed I was told more than once, "You need to write a book." Twenty years later here I am, writing my book

In the summer of 2018, my friend, Anita Carmen, president and founder of Inspire Women in Houston, Texas, became a grandmother, and we began to talk and discuss what that looked like for me. With her encouragement and that of Inspire Women, I wrote the book, my book.

My niece, Jill Mathis Smethurst, brought her two darlings to their first Nana Camp in 2018 (the only two little ones invited outside my eight) and insisted that we write the book. So, I tackled this project with the encouragement of Jill! (Grandma Odia would be so proud!)

I am fully aware that this book is not for everyone. Not every woman will be a grandmother because it is simply not in God's personal plan. But every woman had one! My reflections might lead to some appreciation for the grandmother she had. Not every grandmother will appreciate my approach, because there are as many great ideas as there are grandmothers. My two were certainly very different, and both contributed greatly to my life.

When encouraged to write my thoughts into a book, I certainly had no inclination to write a definitive book on "how to." I would never presume to tell another grandmother what is right or wrong or question her approach. In fact, I find it fascinating to watch how grandmothers operate with their own progeny. Their ideas and excursions have blessed me. Even when they choose to have a minimal involvement in their grandchildren's lives for whatever reason (distance, time, personal priorities, etc.) it is interesting to see how that works out.

I have had so many people ask me, "what do you think?" "What do you do?" "What would you suggest?"

So, for this book, I settled on "my story." ("This is my story! This is my song!")

This is simply my story, my ideas, and my approach to embracing one of the great adventures of my life, being Nana!

Marsha Griffith Eckermann
2020

Acknowledgements

✶ ✶ ✶

To Grandmother Odia, who lived the life and showed me how to "grandmother" simply because of what she was to me.

To L.D, my faithful partner. Without his support I simply could not do what I do.

To Anita, who first planted the idea of my writing a book. I appreciate her constant words of encouragement as she fulfills her ministry's mission statement to "help each woman find her destiny in Christ."

To Jill, who said, "let's do it." Her encouragement was a driving motivation to tell the story of Nana Camp. She nudged me with her comment regarding her two little girls that "the lessons of Nana Camp seep into their souls."

To Joan, the first grandmother to tell me about her "Camp Grammy."

To Reg, the first one to read the book. I appreciate his encouragement as he read and reread and learned what he would do with his daughter's children someday.

To Judy, who lived my childhood with me. I appreciate her constant love and support throughout our lives and her red pen as she, the journalist, corrected my grammar.

To Cathy, my lifelong friend since elementary school. I am very grateful to her for her encouragement and insights. She took my efforts and turned them into something that made more sense to the reader by asking the really hard questions.

To Jane, "Memow," who applied her critical eye and her wisdom to the editing of this book. She has walked many miles with me, often on her knees, and has given my children and grandchildren the gift of her love.

To Karen, who became a mentor and cheerleader in the task of publishing. I appreciate her helping me "make it across the finish line."

To the prayer warriors who pray and gather on Tuesday mornings. Their prayers have provided a barrage of supplications as the Lord has directed the process of writing.

To Caroline, David and T.J., my children who survived their childhoods and love me still. I appreciate their reciprocal love for their mother and the permission they have given her to be part of their children's lives. It is my great joy.

To Jason, Melissa and Emily, who partner with my children in being wonderful parents and who, like their spouses, invite me into these children's lives. They are raising and launching amazing children. They are rich blessings to me.

Nana Camp

Introductions

★ ★ ★

The key players in this unfolding drama are, of course, my grandchildren. In order to follow the story better, let me introduce my children (underlined) and grandchildren.

Jason (R.E. IV) and **Caroline** Griffith Janes
    Jackson Quint Janes   2001
    Joshua Dale Janes   2003
    Jacob Martin Janes   2007
    Joseph Greer Janes   2009

David Martin and Melissa Nichols Griffith
    Hunter James Griffith   1998
    Lily Ann Griffith   2005

Thomas Jonathan and Emily Pylant Griffith
    Georgia Lee Griffith   2009
    Genevieve Jeane Griffith   2013

Chapter 1

The Grandparent Bond (Odia)

★ ★ ★

I grew up in a safe, comfortable loving home. Galveston was not far so we could enjoy the beach. Houston was full of exciting things including the rodeo, the zoo, and parades down Main Street. But my favorite place to go was to Grandmother's house.

It was a simple cottage home in the east end on the corner of York St. and Texas Ave. It had two bedrooms and a small front porch. It was neither lavish nor resplendent. So why did I love to go to Grandmother's house?

Because **she** was there. She created for us an environment that was so full of love and acceptance that one could breathe a little more deeply and sleep a little more soundly in a small bed with a brother or cousin beside you. Grandma Odia, whom we lovingly called Grandmother as the years passed, was not perfect—far from it. But she lived her life before us and welcomed us in to the everyday events.

She did not hide from us her dilemmas as they came: the young mentally disabled girl who would come to the front door and wait until Grandmother called her mother to come get her. The hobo who would politely wait while Grandmother prepared a plate of food for him—and then go back to the train tracks and jump on another train. The "old people" who died in her home. We would realize later that these were all relatives who found great comfort in her presence and literally died in her arms. In the church where she was so active, Grandmother nestled us on her lap, where we often went to sleep, while she listened to the Word of God being taught.

We saw life unfold and watched her deal with it, and with people—in hospitals, at funerals, in the pews, in her kitchen.

My Grandmother was extravagant with her resources. As I have embraced opportunities with my grandchildren, I realized that she did not have many, but we thought we were rich. And we were. Rich in experience. She allowed my cousin, Judy, and me to play with her beloved collection of china dolls. We would make long processions of wedding attendees across her living room floor, and now each of us (as well as her grandchildren and great grandchildren) have those dolls in our homes to remind us of her commitment to us. She allowed Cousin Judy and I to take her best stainless steel pots and pans into the backyard to "cook"—with mud and water. She made our mothers' shared wedding dress, and years later allowed us to dress up in it. Wow! How I would love to have had that wedding dress some years later when I could have worn it for real. All of these fun activities that we enjoyed in her home served to create the platform that she created from which she spoke her powerful lessons of love, acceptance, and Jesus. Dolls, pots and pans, our mothers' wedding dress were all expressions of her love for us. Though we didn't figure it out at the time, she had created that platform from which to speak.

Now, many grandmothers would not approve of such, and I appreciate that. Many grandmothers teach their grandchildren to respect property and touch "with only one finger." That is great. For us, Grandma Odia's extravagance gave us the place to learn the many lessons she had to offer.

Extravagance is not a prerequisite and is not always possible. I know of grandparents who take their grandchildren on cruises, to Disneyland, on great trips around the world. Such trips are fabulous! I share stories with my friend, the grandfather who has "Camp Pops." (We will hear about the "camping" experience later.) While the children's mothers shop with his wife, HE takes the grandchildren on extravagant excursions: to France to the "band of brothers" tour, to Mount Rushmore, to Alaska and Canada. Many grandparents can do that; most cannot. A simple trip to Grandmother's house, in my case, Nana's house, is filled with adventures in her own backyard or kitchen. An adventure budget can be very conservative.

Grandmothers (and grandfathers) create community; my cousins were as close to us as my brothers. Grandmother gave us a place to be together as we grew up. Close, protected, free to be ourselves and know each other.

> ***Prayer:*** Lord, create in my home a place where my grandchildren can come and receive a blessed place of peace and comfort. Give them here a place to be quiet and find the place where You can speak to them and meet their needs.

> ***Prayer:*** Let them meet their cousins here so they can know each other.

At 74 years old I can still feel to my toes the presence of my grandmother. I sit at her feet and play. I watch her deal with pain and suffering. I go to the hospital with her (today I am very comfortable in hospital settings). I watch her teach that Sunday School class (she affectionately called them her "Daisies"). I hear her sing songs of worship as she bangs offkey on her piano. They are vivid memories to me. On Easter Sunday my cousin, Judy, sent me a video of a group singing the hymn, "*oh, how marvelous, oh, how wonderful, and my song shall every be....*" She said, "can't you just hear Grandma Odia bellowing out this song?" Yes, I could. I hope that my grandchildren will have instilled in their souls such feelings of their grandmother. I want the impact not to be about me, but about the Savior Who makes me what I am. I want my relationship with them to be a platform on which I model His love, His acceptance, and His process of knowing Him and surrendering to Him.

I wanted to be with her when the Lord called Odia home. I was not given that privilege. She died alone. He gave her that very private moment without those grandchildren whose lives she had touched, loved, and molded. Thank you, Great God, for Odia Ione McDavid Holtkamp.

My grandmother gave to us a loving grandfather. Grandpa Ernie (Ernest Edwin Holtkamp) was a large, embracing man's man who loved and quoted Bible verses with great authority. He would say in his own words a translation of Proverbs 3:12, "'*whom the Lord loves He chastens...*' and He must be crazy about me." With all of his presence he supported Odia which meant he was the "provider" for us.

Grandfathers assume a critical role in this great scheme. They are the ultimate providers, symbolizing

God's perfect logistical provision for us. We watch them go off to work and come home faithfully. Grandmothers often remind the grandchildren to thank their grandfathers. My grandchildren and I have often written to Poppy, my husband, notes of appreciation for underwriting our adventures.

Grandmother Odia was the obvious person I remember from her generation. Later my mother and dad would become wonderful grandparents.

My mother, Carole Holtkamp Mathis, affectionately called Nanny, was so excited when she became a grandmother with the birth of my daughter, Caroline. Her help, support and encouragement to me was priceless. She came to my house for two weeks with the birth of each of my children, and taught me by her presence that "I could do this thing." This first grandchild was named after her. Though many miles separated us, she called to talk to her baby girl every week and sent her an outfit just as regularly.

My dad was Pawpaw. He was also vice president of a large bank in Houston. Every Christmas he would welcome me and my children into his office. The tradition of riding the bus into downtown Houston, eating at James Coney Island, attending the Texas Commerce Bank choir in the lobby are all part of the memories. However, the simple presence of Martin Mathis in that office was both powerful and comforting. His grandchildren saw an example that has been perpetuated in their lives as adults. The head of the family, providing for each one with a strong presence in his profession, is an example for all to follow. Today he would be proud of his sons and grandsons who are following his legacy. There are two great grandsons who are studying business and hearing the story of their great grandfather.

Then it was my turn to step into that wonderful role. The question had already been settled in God's economy of who their grandfather would be, a surprise to me, but not to my God. My children's father was a wonderfully honorable man who went to be with the Lord in a military plane crash. They were young; Caroline, 10, David, 7 and T.J. just 1. Their children never knew him but know they have a Grandpa Jerry in heaven home. That promise of eternity is his legacy to them, and a powerful one it is: the promise of an eternal heavenly home.

In 1995 Lawrence Dale Eckermann came into our lives. In God's timing I can appreciate the intricacy of the timing. We married shortly before my children married and began their families. L.D. lovingly became Poppy. He is like many grandfathers who offer that large cozy lap where little ones can wrap up and feel the love and comfort of strength and acceptance. In this life they have their Poppy. My God in His perfect plan provided for my grandchildren, the right grandfather for them, Lawrence Dale.

Our story is the perfect testimony of Romans 8:28. That which we would have never wanted, God directed. He worked it all together for good, and we are blessed by the grandfather who shares this great adventure with me. He brings joy to our eight and they bring great joy to him.

There are also the great lessons of wisdom and guidance to learn from grandfathers. One step removed from father, the Grandfather can offer wisdom and direction with a sense of experience as he watches the child growing into adulthood. How many grandfathers have offered that financial helping hand to launch one into his destiny? I love this part of the legacy.

Our culture today often honors grandparents in many ways. Most schools have "Grandparents' Day" where they are honored. All of my grandchildren have shared this day with L.D. and me in their schools. They honor grandparents in the most creative manner and it is a very thoughtful recognition. They write papers, draw pictures, and sometimes read tributes to their grandparents. One year at Jacob's school the question to answer was: "Why should your grandparent run for president?" His answer: "Because she likes to stand up and talk in front of people." The question always comes to my mind, "what do they know about me?" I have kept the stories from school that they have written and their "favorite things to do with Nana and Poppy." That makes me stop and reflect on what I WANT them to know about me. It's a good exercise to consider.

We will leave a legacy whether we realize it or not. Our very presence in their geneology demands a testimony of what we were all about. We don't have a choice. Our grandchildren will seek to know what we left for them to know about us.

I would encourage any grandmother to take time to intentionally define what she wishes her grandchildren to remember about her. We are often encouraged to define our life's mission statement. What is important to you? What do you want to accomplish in your life? What do you want included in your obituary? For the Christian, what do you want to present to the Lord when you stand before Him?

You may never share it with anyone, but it is surely an understanding between you and the Lord. The only prerequisite is to be brutally honest with yourself. As you continue to grow in knowledge of Scripture and personal relationship with the Lord, you will likely find that you are changing or amending your mission statement to reflect His will for your life. This is surely a sign of spiritual growth as you adjust to God's plan and will for your life.

Now take this idea and convert it to your relationship with your grandchildren. It will be your greatest test of how you are doing as a grandmother. WHAT IS YOUR MISSION STATEMENT?

Chapter 2

A Grandmother's Legacy: Building Spiritual Family Relations

✦ ✦ ✦

"May the Lord bless you… all the days of your life… and may you live to see your children's children." Psalm 128: 5–6

"Children's children are a crown to the aged, and parents are the pride of their children." Proverbs 17:6

When your first born becomes a parent and places his first born in your arms, the "magic" begins. It is a deep love affair unlike any other. He or she makes you a grandmother. This is the moment when you start the journey. At that moment with each of my eight grandchildren I whispered to them: "*This is a covenant between you and me. The Lord bless you and keep you. The Lord make His face shine upon you and be gracious unto you. The Lord lift up His countenance upon you and give you peace.*" Numbers 6:24

I was committing to pray for that child for the rest of my life.

The power of prevailing prayer is the undergirding source of our relationship with God. So, it follows that this would be a critical part of our "grandparenting impact." Praying for grandchildren before they were born (or even conceived) is a joy and comfort when placed in the hands of Almighty God. I prayed for them in the womb. "*In your mother's womb I formed you....*" declares Isaiah 44:2 I never prayed for the specific sex after they were conceived because that is the prerogative of God Himself. There is a wonderful book, "The Miracle of Life," (Wells, Robert and Mary, Gire, Ken and Judy, Zondervan Publishing House, 1993) that I journaled for each of my eight and gave a copy to their mothers. It takes you through each week of life in the womb with a wonderful Bible focus. I wrote my own thoughts and prayers for that little fetus forming under the protective Mighty Hand of God. So when they appeared, it was a moment of praise and thanksgiving.

A grandparent's perspective is quite different from that of a parent. I remember that with so much responsibility in my hands, I was very intense about the process as parent. What a great (and grave!) responsibility. God was gracious to me with my three "babies" who have grown into amazing adults and parents.

Knowing that my children were prepared spiritually

for life as parents gave me peace and excitement to determine my role as grandmother. I wanted to embrace the joy, the relationship and never overstep the bounds of what a grandparent is. I have found it beneficial, fun and affirming to tell my grandchildren about their birth from my eyes. They love to hear the stories. They love the unfolding drama of where we were, where I was, how I raced to get to the hospitals, and the first time I held them. Each story is different and each child is unique. They feel very special and wanted, especially those who had brothers or sisters waiting to welcome them. Even as young adults, they smile when I describe their little bald heads, their black curly hair, their sister holding them for the first time. It never gets old.

It was late in my spiritual walk that I was introduced to the power of the blessing of Numbers 6:24

> *"The Lord bless you and keep you; the Lord make His face to shine upon you and be gracious to you. The Lord lift up His countenance upon you and give you peace."*

This verbal intentional prayer spoken into a life is powerful. When applying this to my grandchildren it is an intentional lasting legacy. Once I embraced its full meaning, I began introducing it to my family at gatherings, prayers before meals, and at other special times. Each person would bless the one next to him and as this began to catch on at our prayers before meals, individuals began to interject their own prayers to the one they were blessing. The children watched this. Often we would put them in the middle of our circle and with hands on their heads speak the words of Numbers 6 into their lives. These are actually prayers on their behalf. It is indeed awesome to see the power of Scripture spoken in the form of blessing.

I knew how powerful this was when my grandsons from Lubbock were very young and we visited my aging mother who was in a wheel chair. They saw her physical limitations, but they also saw her soul. Young Joshua, who was probably eight years old, went over to Nanny when no one was watching and whispered in her ear, "Nanny, the Lord bless you and keep you. It's going to be just fine." Well, this Nana was listening with tears of appreciation in her eyes. My mother was thrilled to receive this from him. What a "hallelujah moment." The Word of God **is** alive and powerful, and this blessing is included in its lasting force, passed down in a room of four generations by an eight-year-old.

How many times have we smiled and celebrated the picture of the first hour of life. First the proud adoring parents. Then the grandparent, with that expression of awe and often raw unattractive emotion caught on camera. We don't even care if we look goofy. It surely won't be the last time we get lost in the youthful joy of a new generation where we lose ourselves. If we only knew then the preposterous things we would do with this little one! But who cares!! We are grandparents.

"A child is born. But this is not just any birth or any child. This birth establishes a new generation. This child signifies the beginning of the future. This new baby brings a transformation, changing an ordinary woman into an extraordinary one.

This one little life will make all the difference in the world—for this child will call you Grandma!" or Nana! ("Grandmothers are a Gift from God," Zondervan Press)

However, first YOU have to have a spiritual life. You can't make this stuff up! Your imagination cannot dream up what God designs for those who follow Him.

> *"Eye hath not seen and ear has not heard—*
> *neither has it entered the heart of man,*
> *all that God has prepared for those who*
> *love Him."* (1 CORINTHIANS 2:9)

Start with Jesus—He is the entrance into the Plan of God.

> *"I am the door, by Me if any man enter*
> *in, he shall be saved."* JOHN 10:9

"God so loved the world that He gave His only begotten Son, that whosoever believeth in Him should not perish, but have everlasting life." JOHN 3:16

"But as many as received Him, to them He gave the right (authority) to become children of God, even to those who believer in His name." JOHN 1:12

"Relationship" is one of the strongest words in the English language. We, as human beings, are created to be in relationship. We are not human beings with a spiritual condition; we are spiritual beings with a human condition! I am not sure who brought to me that concept, but it is powerful. It then stands to reason that as powerful as our human relationships are, our spiritual relations are exponentially more powerful.

I have a relationship with God the Father, God the Son, and God the Holy Spirit. My desire is to invite my grandchildren into each of those relationships. The result will be an abundant life for each of them which is filled with personal human relationships, and in this case, family relationships.

There is much written regarding the manner in which we learn how to live the Christian way of life. It begins at the moment of salvation, that moment when we realize that our sins keep us separated from God. He sent Jesus to die for all sin, and therefore, by putting our faith in His work on the cross we become believers. Many good people will be reading this book who have never stopped to make sure Who they are depending on for eternal salvation. Perhaps their good works are so impressive that they have never considered that they are never good enough. Salvation depends not on any of our good works, but on faith alone in Christ alone. He tells us to *"believe on the Lord Jesus Christ and thou shalt be saved."* Acts 16:31

"For as many as received Him, to then He gave the right to become children of God, even to those who believe in His name." John 1:12

We are not left to our own devices or imagination on how to know and please God, not for salvation, not for living the Christian life. On the contrary, He is very specific in how we, as Christians, approach Him, know Him and please Him. The scriptures tell us that there is a way that seems right to man, and after that the judgment. Judges 17:6 says that *"every man did right in his own eyes."* This suggests that God was not impressed. They were pleasing themselves, not Him. He requires our obedience, and that means we have to know what to obey. The Christian life is provided by God for us to live in rich blessing if we obey Him and His provision. The children of Israel constantly disobeyed His way, were disciplined and brought back into obedience. They often learned the hard way what this relationship with God looked like.

This tells us that He has specific guidelines He wants us to know to live this abundant life. *"I came that they might have life, and might have it more abundantly."* John 10:10. So it stands to reason that these guidelines are not a secret. They are clearly stated in His Word. I prefer to call these guidelines "protocols."

His Word is the key to living and executing this great adventure called the Christian way of life. Without the guidelines, or protocols, in which to operate in the Christian life, we just don't. My prayer is for my grandchildren to get those tools from God's Word.

"The Word of God is alive and powerful, sharper than any two-edged sword." Hebrews 4:12

There is a well-defined protocol for living the spiritual life that glorifies God. "Protocol" is a precisely defined procedure. It involves a life of fellowship with God, faith, loving God's Word, service to others, and understanding the power of God's Spirit in us. **This is the great message** I desire to pass on to my grandchildren one principle at a time, and to pray for their parents as they teach them. Often, I pray for other people who will cross their paths (teachers, coaches, friends, etc) who will speak into their lives timeless Truths. These truths are not always received from grandparents or parents. They may often be received through another person that the Lord has prepared. Thank the Lord for that person.

> ***Prayer:*** May you, Lord, give them desire to know Him and His Word.

He is revealed in scripture. 2 Timothy says, "*He (who) was revealed in the flesh, was vindicated in the Spirit, beheld by angels, proclaimed among the nations, believed on in the world, taken up in glory.*"

To lead a child (especially a grandchild) to that Savior is over-the-top. To pray for their parent to be used in this process of evangelism is amazing. Our first desire is for them to know the Savior. The Gospel is the greatest gift we can pass on.

If this seems to you a rather "concrete" approach, perhaps it's because that is the way I have learned to follow the Lord. But it is much more than learn-and-apply. It is actually the heart and soul of knowing the Lord Jesus Christ. God's entire plan for man is revealed in Jesus. He executed the salvation plan on the cross. He is revealed in the Word of God and through the power of the Holy Spirit. He not only shows us the **how** of living, but the **Who**. Getting to know Jesus results in a growing love for Him and the proof of that love—the yielding to God's Holy Spirit through obedience.

A great example He gives to us is "*abiding in the vine.*" John 15:1–10. Jesus is the vine; we are the branches.

As the branch gets constant nourishment from the vine, so we get that nourishment from Jesus as we grow in grace in the power of the Holy Spirit and the knowledge of the Word of God. One leads to the other. *"If you abide in Me as my Words abide in you, ask what you wish, and it shall be done unto you."* John 15:7 That is a description of a beautiful relationship between Father God and His child. We don't make up the conditions for this relationship. He does, and He gives them to us as protocols, as specific guidelines for living the abundant life.

Another example is the shepherd and the sheep. Sheep are secure and safe with the shepherd. Their every need is met because the shepherd is leading them. They have no need to fear because their shepherd is strong. They have no fear because they know how this works. Sheep know the protocol! For them it exists in the shepherd's voice. They are secure inside the sheepfold and in obedience to the shepherd's voice. If they wander or revolt, they are in trouble. How do they know what to do? They listen for the shepherd's call and return to him or they wait for him to find them. The shepherd has given them secure boundaries. They are safe as long as they remain and abide within those boundaries.

Now, once I live in this momentum of abiding which leads to a close relationship with my Shepherd, I am ready to pass it on. Once again, I cannot model it to my grandchildren unless I live this life myself. Once they begin understand God's great love for them, learn from God's Word what pleases Him, and rely on the Holy Spirit to guide them, they will experience God's grace in abundant living.

Prayer

Prayer is a critical component to building the spiritual life. "More things are wrought by prayer than this world dreams of," wrote the poet, Tennyson. The Bible tells us how:

Teaching your grandchildren about prayer which includes (1) how to pray, (2) what to pray, (3) the protocols for praying according to God's Word.

Praying **with** them in order to model by example your relationship with God and to include them in this wonderful experience.

Praying **for** them.

Talking to the God of the universe is an incredible blessing for the believer. After praying at the beginning of a board meeting, a friend said to me, "you pray like you know God personally." To this, I answered, "I do." And He has taught me that effective prayer is an expression and extension of the fabric of my soul. He invites me to know Him and approach Him. I love my husband and think about him all day. My relationship with Jesus Christ means I am occupied with Him all day. Prayer must be done according to **His** bidding, yes, according to His designed plan which includes: praying to the Father, through the Son, in the power of the Holy Spirit. Knowing the Great, loving God Who hears our children's prayers brings them into relationship with Him. Of course, this follows their entering into that relationship through salvation. Learning to know this loving heavenly Father is a great adventure, but someone has to give them the introduction and then the information.

When exploring the blessing of prayer, we all need to know that God the Father hears only the prayers of those who have trusted Christ as Savior. He is the mediator between God and man. There are a multitude of ways to teach this to children. In fact, the more we teach them about Jesus, the more they will love Him and want to please Him through their obedience.

The invisible Person of the Godhead, the Holy Spirit, gives us the power to approach God and engage deeper into relationship with Him. This great invisible member of the trinity is an interesting Person to get to know. The wind is a great venue in explaining that He is not seen, but is felt, especially when we respond to Him. Sin breaks our fellowship with Him and His power is cut off. But confession restores it.

> *"If we confess our sins He is faithful and just to forgive us our sins and to cleanse us from all unrighteousness."* 1 JOHN 1:9

Restored fellowship is a grace provision that gives great momentum to the Spiritual life.

For generations my family has been committed to the power of prayer by praying for each other. The internet and the cell phone have made this an easier opportunity. Oh, the health challenges, the deaths, the problems, large and small that we have shared and taken immediately to the Throne of Grace and have been answered by God's perfect will and plan. It is a blessing to me to watch the next generation take up this powerful weapon. They all know that there is a band of committed prayer warriors ready to take their request before the Father.

Prayer has become as normal as the air we breathe. The purpose here is not to explain the intricacies of this rich prayer life, but we must understand what it is. It does no good to pray outside of the plan that is put forth for us to approach Him. So teaching is the first step.

My mentor, Jeannette, modeled for me a beautiful practice. No matter where we were, if someone asked her to pray for them, she would stop right there and address the Father, sometimes with her eyes closed. It mattered not how many people were in the room. She interceded many times this way for me and mine.

The legacy of Barbara Green, mother of Steve Green, founder of the Museum of the Bible, is a powerful testimony to the power of prevailing prayer. Her daughter-in-law, Jackie Green writes: "Steve and his siblings all have their favorite stories of instances when, in difficult times, their mother pointed them to prayer rather than worry. She not only preached this; she modeled it. She prayed each of her children into the kingdom of God through a genuine, personal relationship with Jesus Christ. She prayed them through the sometimes-perilous teen years. She also prayed the whole family through the risk-filled arduous years of launching Hobby Lobby from the family's garage." (Green, Jackie and McAfee, Lauren Green, "Only One Life: How a Woman's every day Shapes an Eternal Legacy," Zondervan, 2018, p. 212)

When our second grandson, Jackson, was just a small tyke (maybe 6), he was happy to pray at the dinner table. His mom and I had been praying for him as he was presented the Gospel of Jesus Christ. We were just waiting to hear his faith in his own words. One evening she called and said with sheer joy, "I got it! I heard it." Jackson was going to say the prayer at dinner and he began, "God the Father, I want to make sure I go to heaven so I trust Jesus as my Savior… and thank you for the food." Now that's a prayer—one that will have eternal repercussions. Way to go, Jackson.

Joe, who was about 5 at the time, was in the backseat of the car one afternoon while I was driving the four boys home from a movie about Jerusalem. Of course, we engaged in a deep theological discussion which led to Heaven. One by one the boys said, "I have trusted in Jesus." And Joe, from his car seat said, "well, I have not." So, we said, "well, you can do that right now." While Nana almost drove off the road with joy, I led him in a simple prayer of faith whereby he trusted the Lord Jesus Christ as his Savior. Those are the prayers you will never forget! It comes very naturally for us.

I learned to listen carefully to their words and to trust the Lord with their spiritual conversions. One day while Georgia, Genny, and I were playing with American girl dolls, Genny, who was then about four years old, was swinging on the four-poster bed. She casually announced, "Jesus died for all the children." My ears perked up and we talked all about that, concluding that He died for **her**. An unexpected moment turned into a revelation about our Savior.

Josh (#3) was a prolific prayer warrior as soon as he could speak. As a little one he would go on and on as the food grew cold until Dad said, "and thank You for the food."

Building family relations involves encouraging connection. That gift of prayer will conncct a family, for sure. I have a very strong connection and bond with my cousins and with my family. My mother was the link; my grandmother was the link. I have eight grandchildren; I am the link between these cousins. You are the link between your children and their children, the cousins, your grandchildren.

Grandmothers have the most creative ways to encourage community. Holiday gatherings, summer vacations, and Nana Camp (coming up in chapter 4) have been great for us. I see cousins forming lasting relationships because of the family they share.

My brothers, cousins, and I grew up together to appreciate this bond. Now our children and grandchildren have formed their relationships as the gatherings continue. I am delighted to see second and third cousins "discovering" each other and the ancestors they share.

My grandchildren love their cousins. They still plan their vacations every summer just to be together. Not only are my husband and I committed, so are my brothers and their wives. We gather for reunions every year at the beach. We watch those cousins and second cousins and third cousins come together to know each other and the content of their legacy. Their relationship with the Lord has continued for six generations. My commitment is to trust the Lord and accept my assignment to carry it on.

In compiling my thoughts, I have learned from so many examples of those who have established this familial bond. I read about adult brothers and their sister who are raising their families in a neighborhood near their grandparents in Houston. The cousins see each other and play together every day; and the brothers and sister call upon each other to help with their individual families. Those grandparents did a great job of forming community.

Then there are those huge family reunions which take place on ranches and farms. They gather by the generations and stay for days to eat, laugh, and have hayrides. That is a great venue. Good job, parents who started this. And the stories go on and on.

Frances Weaver says, "growing up in Kansas, my sisters and I needed only to cross the street to go to Grandmother's. She lived in the old Victorian where my father and his six sisters had been raised. I sat on the same front porch, ate at the same table, played in the same attic, slept on the same sleeping porch, explored the same fruit cellar, swung under the same tree, and swiped the same soft ginger cookies my dad had thrived on. My cousins—some from as far away as Illinois or California—adored Grandmother and her cookies, too, but I believed the proprietary rights were mine." ("Grandmothers…", p25.)

Alan Wright shares a beautiful story when a matriarch in his church died and her granddaughter shared some thoughts. "When I was a little girl, while other children were going to Disneyworld, I was going to Grandma's house. We would pack up the car in Tampa wave to Mickey Mouse on the way past Orlando, and head north. And I thought I was the luckiest kid in the world. My grandmother's house was the most comforting, interesting, exciting place to be on earth. The lightning bugs were brighter there at night; the breeze cooler from the front porch swing; the cantaloupe sweeter in the refrigerator. Someone else now lives at 921 West Street and I, along with all my cousins, only have memories of the house where Grandma lived, but that is Okay. It is just fine. Because… as I sit with my son on my lap, and seek to instruct and shepherd his heart, using the same phrases as my Grandmother, I know that the home my Grandmother built will live on through the legacy of her life and her influence." (Wright, Alan, "Sharing the Light Ministry"). Wow! That would be a great blessing for my grandchildren to have such memories.

There are throughout history great family dynasties that flourish and encourage each other. Bravo.

Stewart Morris is a founding father of Houston Baptist University in Houston, Texas. In 2018 his 99th birthday was celebrated and his statue dedicated on the campus. Three generations of his family gathered to dedicate that statue. Three generations who support that Christ-centered University. Three generations who make an impact on the lives of students who attend HBU. Three generations who remember the impact of their grandmother, Joella Morris who is now with the Lord.

Nana Camp

Jenna Bush Hager has shared with us the legacy left to her by her two grandmothers, First Lady Barbara Bush and Jenna Welch. Cindy Burnett, staff writer for the "Bellaire Buzz" in Houston, Texas, reviewed her book, "Everything Beautiful in Its Time: Seasons of Love and Loss." Mrs. Hager "shared their words and wisdom with family and friends and they urged her to memorialize these anecdotes in a book. Hager uses various formats including letters to her grandparents she wishes she could tell them." Mrs. Hager paints a picture of two very different grandmothers who had profound influence on her life.

A few years ago we as a nation watched the large family dynasty who for generations have lived their lives in service to our nation. George H.W. Bush was celebrated the second week of December, 2018. The nation watched three generations honor their father and celebrate his faith. We saw the picture of five generations who have richly the blessed the life of America. I especially loved the grandchildren who spoke of Grampy, and thanked the Lord for the life of a grandfather (and grandmother). Not all families live on such a large scale.

We were privileged to see this American dynasty on the big screen. Not all of us have such visible impact. Much was learned from watching that memorial to a president. As the grandchildren spoke, I was impressed time and again of the impact of grandparents. One grandson spoke of a time of personal (and public) failure that were met with the kind and gracious words from his grandfather who encouraged him to recover and move on. Those personal messages from a beloved grandfather made a difference in his life which is now one of public service. Many spoke of the letters they would receive from their grandfather—handwritten with intimate words of love, wisdom, and encouragement. Great example for all grandparents.

As I look at the many ways a grandparent can make the difference in a life, three great protocols come to mind: pray, encourage, live.

Our prayers undergird the spiritual. Encouragement is powerful. The greatest legacy we can give our loved ones is simply living the spiritual life of obedience to Christ and walking in the Spirit. Some call it "walking the walk." When they look at us may they see a life of surrender and obedience to the Lord where we use the spiritual dynamics He has given us every day.

> ***Prayer:*** Help me live my life in faithful obedience to You. May my grandchildren see my faith, my love for Jesus Christ, my obedience to Your Work, and my walk in the power of the Holy Spirit. May they see my application of the walk clearly so they will know what to do.

> *Prayer:* On the landscape of human history, let my life count as I seek to glorify Him and promote His Kingdom.

When my dear friend, Dr. E.D. (Doug) Hodo was diagnosed with cancer he told his family, "I have taught you how to live. Now I will show you how to die." And he did! Doug Hodo was the second president of Houston Baptist University. His life was marked by obedience to the Word of God which he taught clearly and service to Jesus Christ. The relationships he had with his family, and specifically, his grandchildren, will extend into eternity. Do I hear a "hallelujah?"

> *Prayer:* When dying grace comes, may they see my relationship with Jesus and surrender to Him until the very end.

> *Prayer:* May they be encouraged to know that eternity awaits me and then because they have believed on the Lord Jesus Christ for salvation, awaits them.

Parents will value and appreciate the support of such a grandparent. I recently heard a voice on a radio program discussing family values saying, "use your secret weapon, the grandmother." I wish I knew who said this so I could give them credit, but they are very wise!! With a smile, I tuned in and heartily agreed. A grandparent serves in a support role for the parent. Defining that role is important. All must understand the role the grandmother assumes making the parent comfortable. Once all have understood the role and the assignments (including boundaries) the invitation to "come on board" is music to the ears. The basics can be reinforced by the grandparent: chores, cooking, diet, clean up, family history, and the Word of God! For many, these life lessons are ends in themselves. For me, they are platforms to present the greater objective: knowing Jesus.

"I wonder if Grandma, in all her simplicity, wasn't a more effective evangelist than the world's greatest preachers." (Southard, Betty anad Stoop, Jan, "Grandmothers are a Gift from God," Zondervan Press, p. 23)

> ***Prayer:*** prepare me with the tools and insights of Your Word to live a life worthy of a legacy. I know that it can only be done through You.

My mentor, Jeannette Clift George, used to say that the best thing you can do is "just show up." That could include just showing up at the hospital, a funeral, a wedding, the sick bed, a performance, and certainly, as grandmother, into the life of your grandchild. Often your words don't matter, just show up. Those grandchildren will never forget that you were there.

Creating a strong family bond translates into relations that are closely knit for a lifetime. This includes brothers, sisters, aunt, uncles, and cousins! In my family the first link for cousins to know and love each other is the grandmother! My brothers and I are close to our three maternal cousins because, while our parents kept us together; our grandmother's house is where we met most of the time. Our memories are priceless. Today I have the greatest loving support from all of these with whom I grew up and have lived my life. We have been in each other's weddings. We have sat in hospital rooms. We have buried our parents and spoken at those services. I know that they will always "have my back." And every holiday finds us in close touch with each other.

My niece, Jill, grew up with her cousins (my children). While writing this book, she shared with me that she always thought that "those are the coolest humans." She is still close to them and now her daughters are best friends with my two youngest granddaughters. The second cousins see each other in close community. That's thanks to their grandmothers!

In a radio discussion, Chuck Swindoll, author, speaker, president of "Insight for Living" defines the book of Deuteronomy in four words, and I would add a fifth:

> Hear… God's voice
> 4:36, 6:4
> Love… the Lord with all your heart
> 6:5, 10:12, 30:16
> Teach… God's Word
> 4:10, 11:19
> Fear… the Lord reverently
> 3:22, 6:2
> Obey… the Lord and His statutes
> 4:40, 5:27, 6:17, 28:1

This serves as a great outline for building strong spiritual bonds when all are following these directives. God admonished Israel, "*…that you and your son and your grandson might fear the Lord your God, to keep all His statutes and His commandments, which I command you all the days of your life.*" Deuteronomy 6:2.

Nana Camp

> ***Prayer:*** May I be the example of hearing Your advice through Your Word, of loving in joyful excess, smiling, inviting others to join the party! of teaching my grandchildren, of fearing You with no dread, but with an awesome respect, of obeying you in surrender.

> ***Prayer:*** May my theology be my biography.

Strong family relations are built one generation at a time. One of our favorite family times actually occurred when my youngest brother, Mark, had suffered from Guillian Barre syndrome, a debilitating condition that left him paralyzed for a time. The year was 2006, and our family was jolted by this sudden trial. As soon as he was diagnosed, his siblings (myself included), nephews, nieces, and cousins raced to Houston to join his wife and children. It was a trying time when everyone surrounded that family to offer medical assistance, financial advice, business support, love and, of course, lots of prayer. Mark **did** recover and has little lingering affect.

His daughter's wedding was scheduled during the time of his recovery where all of the family attended and spoke for Mark. His testimony was strong and amazing as he simply trusted His Lord to heal him. The result of that testimony was an awakening, a revival, some would say. Hunter was then eight years old and was growing in his young faith. He told his dad, our son, David, that he wanted to be baptized. So, his Dad asked if he wanted to do that in their church or would he like to be baptized during the family week at the beach. Guess what he decided?

David quickly asked me to organize a "family baptism" that summer, and ask Uncle Mark if he would do the honors. When I went to the hospital to ask, he just laughed and answered, "well, I would be honored—IF I can **walk**!." Walk, he did.

As the Lord would have it, there was a large group of our family who had never been baptized, saved but not baptized. And that's another story. On a glorious day in Galveston with the sun shining, we had a service of worship and prayer on the beach. Then eight members of my family walked into the Gulf of Mexico with Uncle Mark and two strong young soldiers, of the next generation, his son and one of mine, walking beside him in case he needed a little help. Yes, there were tears of joy, especially as I watched my three children and my oldest grandson profess their faith in Jesus Christ and receive baptism. I was amazed at the desire of these four other family members. Yes, another Hallelujah moment!

And on the shore in her wheelchair with her caregiver beside her was my mother; a mother, grandmother, great grandmother watching a profound moment Thank you, Lord. I can only imagine the many prayers and discussions emanating from her soul over the year as she witnessed her legacy continuing in the lives of her descendants.

My mother had a deep personal relationship with Jesus Christ. She had an enduring love for His Word. She passed this on to her children and her grandchildren. She would love to see that passed on to her great grandchildren. That which was so strong in her soul, she passed on.

Building a legacy of strong family relationships is a process. It doesn't take place over night; it develops over years of careful attention through prayer, personal interaction, and taking note of what the Lord is doing in each life. It helps if we stay available to our beloved grandchildren! In that way, we create a platform which allows us to "pass it on."

Chapter 3

Pass It On—a Command from Scripture

★ ★ ★

Introduction (what is a legacy?)

Psalm 78:3–5. *"...our fathers have told us. We will not conceal them from their children. But tell (pass on) to the generation to come the praises of the Lord, and His strength and His wonderous works that He has done."*

This is a command to "pass it on." It is not a suggestion.

Webster's Dictionary, 1960 edition, defines legacy as *anything handed down from, or as from, an ancestor to a descendant.*

A simple definition holds within its scope something very powerful. What is created in one person's life is handed down to another. Legacies handed down, whether monetary or not, have literally changed the life of the recipient.

So, for our purposes, this definition begs several questions. **What** are we passing on? Why would our grandchildren care what we have to offer? Since you cannot create a platform from which to pass on a legacy without your commitment and presence in their lives, do we show up? **Why** do they want to come to us in the first place?

These children of ours are links in a long line of believers who are used in the Plan of God throughout the history of man. The great river flowing through time is a meaningful visual for me. As Franklin Graham said on television, "We take only one dip into that river." Beginning with the first parents in the garden, history has been passed from one person to the next. God doesn't zap us in and out of history. He gives us parents who train us. He gives us children to pass on the line. We may enjoy a life of many generations before us, or we may know only our parents, but we can rest assured that we are links that are critical to the passage of time and God's plan for the ages.

> *"Know therefore that the Lord your God is God; He is the faithful God, keeping His covenant of love to a thousand generations of those who love Him and keep His commands."* DEUTERONOMY 7:9

> *"I will open my mouth in parables, I will utter hidden things, things from of old—what we have heard and known, what our fathers have told us. We will not hide them from their*

children; we will tell the next generation the praiseworthy deeds of the Lord, His power, and the wonders He has done." PSALM 78:2–4

Our time on earth can count for something with eternal results—or it can count for little of eternal value.

> ***Prayer:*** Teach me to be part of your eternal purpose and may my grandchildren know and embrace this legacy.

I love to think of the woman from centuries ago who drew water from a well, or the one, generations later, who pumped water from the ground. I am related to them, and they could only imagine a granddaughter centuries later who would turn on a kitchen faucet for her water.

Every generation will stand on its own in regard to the challenges it will meet and endure in the history of time. Some will begin great adventures as did the Pilgrims and Puritans of Plymouth and Jamestown. Some will live their lives in slavery. Some will fight great wars for freedom. It is no accident that the generation from the 1940s would be referred to as "the greatest generation". We cannot live the destiny that was our fathers' and mothers'. We cannot face the challenges that our grandchildren will face, but we can impact our time and help with their preparation!

During the writing of this book, the world is in the middle of the COVID-19 pandemic. Queen Elizabeth II addressed her nation with the hope that those who come after her would find that she and her people stood strong and "did it well." This lady has left a powerful legacy, both personally and as queen. History will reveal her story of over 100 years and her testimony during the pandemic. She was also a grandmother who had great influence with her "royal" grandchildren. She surely leaves them a legacy.

During this pandemic, the voices of wisdom can be heard across our nation. One need only to listen. While cities burn, grandmothers are speaking lessons of hope to their grandchildren. They are reminding the next generations of the wisdom from God to discern hope and offer bastions of security. It is also a great time to pray for our children as they make difficult decisions concerning theirs.

John F. Kennedy spoke these words on January 20, 1961 in his inauguration speech: *"in the long history of the world, only a few generations have been granted her role of redefining freedom in its hour of maximum danger. I do not shrink from this responsibility. I welcome it. I do not believe that any of us would exchange places with any other people of any other generation. The energy, the faith, the devotion which we bring to this endeavor will light our country and all who serve it, and the glow from that fire can truly light the world…. ASKING His blessing and His help, but knowing that here on earth God's work must truly be our own."*

Whether or not these words of blessing were fulfilled in his time or in the next generation is for the historian to decide. In the "long history of the world" it is certain that many generations have done the work of God, and many have not. Your grandchildren will live in their own unique time and will make their stand one way or another.

You and I have the privilege of being part of their preparation.

The many opportunities I have found to demonstrate this message of hope include Nana Camp (coming up in the next chapter!), holiday gatherings, beach vacations, and every single time I am with them!

It is also helpful to define the legacy that was passed on to you. It is a great exercise to explore the messages that were given to you along the way by your parents and grandparents. Some will want to gently blow them away as false. If they don't line up with the Scripture you know, put it aside. For some they will want to intentionally and powerfully reject the evil, harm, or destructive messages that were spoken into their souls by a grandparent. We have often called on the Lord to deliver folks from strongholds or evil trends that were passed down generations ago. These strongholds can embrace our children when they are not even aware. The enemy would love to keep us in the dark, confused in bondage to our family sins. Liberating these strongholds, seeing them for what they are and claiming victory is freedom in Jesus. Cleaning out the bad stuff is often a powerful gift we can give our grandchildren.

With knowledge of doctrine from the Word of God, which teaches us God's ways, our grandchildren can be liberated from bondage and learn how to avoid repeating it. Knowledge is power! God is always victorious when His Word is applied.

The most powerful message that we can pass on as our legacy is the blessing, the Gospel, the Presence of Jesus. Our grandchildren will see this when we walk with Him, operate from the power of the Holy Spirit and the doctrine in our souls, and answer with the Truth that is in us. When our grandchildren bring us questions or dilemmas they will come with the confidence that we will know answers formed from the Word of God. Remember, you can't make this up as you go along.

> *Prayer:* let the content of my heart show that Jesus is living there.

To this prayer request and public statement, my daughter-in-law answered, "she is real, you can't fake this stuff." He IS real. You could never make this up. It's the great blessing God has in store.

My grandmother Odia introduced me to The Lord Jesus Christ. My mother, Carole, gave me a love for His Word. My legacy is a powerful one.

"A righteous man who walks in his integrity—how blessed are his sons after him." PROVERBS 20:7

I am grateful to be the product of women who went before me and walked with integrity. What does that mean when I think of Odia, Carole and Mary Lou (my aunt)? I am influenced by women who though very human and not perfect, were believers in Jesus Christ and walked in obedience to His Word. I know the stories of their salvation—all as little girls. I know and saw the power of their study of the Word and their lives of walking in the light of that Word. There is absolutely no substitute for studying the Word of God under a pastor-teacher who knows Jesus personally and has studied His Truth. My family's Bibles are marked. The Word was the fabric of their souls. They passed on to the next generation the invitation to "come and join me...." There is only one way, and they made it very clear.

The Greatest Legacy Opportunity

The purpose, the goal, the focus, the great message of Truth is passed from one person to another. Many people will be used to guide, and speak into the life of a positive prepared believer. What a sense of destiny to be one of those people who teaches the next generation the amazing plan of God as revealed in Jesus Christ.

Remember, this is a command to "pass it on." It is not a suggestion.

My platform is simple: Jesus Christ, and Him crucified. It is important to define our life's "mission statement". Know what and for me, WHO we are passing on You cannot give or pass on what is not inside of you already, so be prepared! For me, that has been a lifetime of knowing Jesus Christ, walking in His Word, building in my soul the power of the Christ-centered life.

Above all, be consistent. Whatever your "message," it will be your legacy. Don't change and confuse your mission statement. Really, our life statement is constant. Mine is simple: Jesus is the all-inclusive answer. It never changes. My prayer is that when you see me, you see Him. When you feel loved by me, it is because I am loved by Him. That simple and that powerful.

> ***Prayer:*** May my grandchildren see the Living Word living in me.

It is a good exercise to prayerfully write out your life's mission statement. You may never share it with anyone, but it is surely an understanding between you and the Lord. The only prerequisite it to be brutally honest with yourself. As you continue to grow in knowledge and personal relationship with the Lord, you will probably find that your mission statement changes or adjusts to newly acquired knowledge from the Word of God. That is surely a sign of spiritual growth.

Then apply that mission statement to your relationship with your grandchildren. It will be your greatest test of how you are doing as a grandmother.

Why a legacy

Paul wrote to Timothy, "*I have been reminded of your sincere faith, which first lived in your grandmother Lois and in your mother Eunice and, I am persuaded, now lives in you also.*" 2 Timothy 1:5

When we are alert, we can find the opportunity to "pass it on" and then see the results of the legacy in the lives of our grandchildren. I count on Him to show me how to be part of this great development through history.

The tamarisk tree is planted in Israel for the generations to come. It grows slowly and offers its greatest provision of shade for the next generation. The traditions of your family are critical. The importance of roots to your grandchildren, especially in today's culture, when people don't know where they come from or who they are, remain important as guides in your grandchild's foundation.

> *Prayer:* May the tree that I am growing today be shade to nurture and comfort the generations to follow. I am counting on you, Lord.

Legacies from the Bible

Joshua 4:21 relates the story of the second crossing of an impossible body of water by the Israelites. This time after they crossed the Jordon into the Promised Land, they were instructed to leave 12 stones as memorials. Now, they remembered the crossing of the Red Sea with Moses. Surely that story was passed down from generation to generation. Can you hear the grandmother relating the experience?

The 12 stones were a memorial to God's faithful Hand, once again, delivering this people. When "the children ask" (verse 21), the fathers are commanded to tell them the story. Tell them about their God. Make sure they know Who He is and what He has done for them. What a perfect example of the command (yes, command) to pass it on. Here we see a format of what to tell them: (1) tell the story, their history; (2) relate the past event (crossing the Red Sea) (3) explain the character of God for He reveals Himself to every generation (I can hear the lessons of the power of God and His great love for them.) (4) tell them their place. (He is with you today. Fear/respect Him. You are His.)

Joshua 21 tells of the children of Israel finally possessing the Promised Land. *"So the Lord gave Israel all the land which He had sworn to give to their fathers, and they possessed it, and lived in it. And the Lord gave them rest on every side, according to all that He had sworn to their fathers."* V. 44,45. Then they were warned, *"only be very careful to observe the commandment and the law which Moses the servant of the Lord commanded you, to love the Lord your God and walk in all His ways and keep His commandments, and hold fast to Him and serve Him with all your heart and with all your soul. So Joshua blessed them and sent them away, and they went to their tents."* V. 5,6.

What a defining moment in the history of Israel! Can you just hear the grandmothers? I can imagine a grandmother explaining to the children the history of their ancestors, their deliverance from slavery, all the lessons learned in the wilderness, and the faithfulness of God. Can you hear her admonishing them to love the Lord and be obedient to His Word? Can you hear her praising Him?

When I think of examples of how to leave a legacy, I am reminded of two men from the Bible (I'm sure there are many women—and specifically grandmothers!). My mentor, Jeannette Clift George, brought them to me with her very personal exhortations. The first is Nicodemus who came to Jesus (John 3:1) with his questions. What Jesus did not do was condemn him for his question. What He DID say was, "ok, I will place Myself at the identity of your confusion." God does not respond to our lack of absolutes with anything but the Truth. He spoke clearly to Nicodemus who might not have understood at the first encounter, but truly embraced the Christ and found his life changed by this encounter.

> ***Prayer:*** May I walk with You and speak clearly your Truth that my grandchildren will hear clearly, watch the evidence unfold in my life, and know this Savior.

> ***Prayer:*** May I never condemn or shame them because of their questions.

> ***Prayer:*** May I always be ready to give wise counsel because of the doctrine in my soul. Make it YOUR counsel, not mine.

The second example is Lazarus. After that earth-shaking, ground-moving miracle of raising him from the dead, Jesus was met with anger and the decision from the religious leaders to kill Him. Of course, there were many who trusted this Messiah/God and became His followers after such a moment. As the story moves to the triumphal entry into Jerusalem at the beginning of "Passion Week," there is Lazarus who is walking with Him. Living, walking proof of His power. This begs the question: "what to do with Lazarus?" Ignore him, reject him, explain away the fact that he was dead? He was actually the living, walking proof of the power of this Jesus Christ—begging seekers to consider this Jesus.

When Jesus said to Thomas, "here's the proof, the nail prints in my hands. Try Me!" it is the resounding call down through history!

> ***Prayer:*** May my life be like Nicodemus, Thomas, and Lazarus, calling to my grandchildren, "I am the proof! Try Him!"

> ***Prayer:*** May I embrace the story of Lazarus, and may my life say, "He makes me live." May they look at me and ask what to do with her Jesus.

One of my mother's favorite bible stories (her legacy to me!!!) is the story of the Exodus and specifically, the bones of Joseph. You will remember the life of Joseph and how he ended up as ruler of Egypt. Because he knew the prophecy that Israel would inherit their promised land, and most important, because he believed it, Joseph told the children of Israel to not bury his bones in Egypt. Remember, they were not yet in slavery. He knew they would become enslaved from the prophecy of God's spoken word. He knew they would be delivered; he claimed this promise. His words taught the faithfulness of God. He always keeps His Word.

So, for 400 years while the Jews were in slavery, after the kings forgot Joseph, the children would ask the question to their fathers, "what is that Egyptian sarcophagus,

Nana Camp

and why is it among us?" It became a powerful training aid. The fathers would then explain who Joseph was, what God had promised, and the reality of God's immutable Word. In the midst of terrible circumstances, many slaves lived and died in chains. But they had the promise represented by the bones of Joseph. Even after his death, Joseph's legacy spoke powerfully to the children of Israel.

Then, as God promised, the day came. (and here my mother would cry!) They marched out of Egypt as free people. *"and Moses took the bones of Joseph with him, for he had made the sons of Israel solemnly swear, saying, 'God shall surely take care of you; and you shall carry my bones from here with you.'* Exodus 13:19

Now, that is victory. That is evidence of God's person, His work, and His promises. We can trust this God. That is the message passed on from one generation to the next for 400 years.

> ***Prayer:*** Lord, let my personal testimony be such that it is remembered for generations. May it reveal Your Person and Your work in my time. May it call my grandchildren and their grandchildren to know and trust you.

> ***Prayer:*** Keep me faithful to Your Word as I apply it now.

Legacy of Prayer

In the previous chapter we discussed the importance of prayer in building Spiritual family relationships. Now let us turn to the importance of making this great tool a part of our legacy.

Exodus 30:6 speaks to me of the command to pass "it" on to the generations. The Lord spoke to Aaron when He established the tabernacle after the Jews were freed from slavery in Egypt: *"and you shall put this altar in front of the veil that is near the ark of the testimony, in front of the mercy seat that is over the ark of the testimony, where I will meet with you… and Aaron shall burn fragrant incense on it; he shall burn it every morning when he trims the lamps. And when Aaron trims the lamps at twilight, he shall burn incense. There shall be perpetual incense before the Lord throughout your generations."*

I love the application that we as church age believers know about the altar of incense—that great article in the tabernacle that sent up incense constantly. That incense represents to me the power of prevailing prayer. Our constant offering of prayer to the Throne of Grace is pictured in the constant lifting of the incense. Oh, the sweet aroma of a grandmother who prays for her grandchildren! When offered according to God's plan and purpose, it is a powerful force in the life of the child.

In every age He promises to "meet with you…" as He did with Aaron and the Israelites.

> ***Prayer:*** May I be faithful in responding to the invitation to meet with You.

I know that my grandmother, and especially my grandfather prayed for me! Remember, Ernest Holtkamp? He was stricken with Parkinson's disease for a major portion of his life. When we visited Houston we would always see him, and I would give him my intimate prayer requests (my husband was in the Air Force during Viet Nam) and I knew that Grandfather would pray.

My mother was my powerful prayer warrior, and now my children call me often with requests for themselves and for their children. May the incense of prayer be offered from your soul as a sweet aroma to the God Who sits on the Throne.

Legacy of the Word of God

The priority of the study of the Bible is an obvious part of my personal legacy. After faith in Christ for salvation, nothing pleases me more than to see the Word of God being applied in the lives of my children and grandchildren.

In a day when the Bible is not as revered as in our nation's past, it becomes our challenge to show these grandchildren how vital and exciting and NECESSARY the Word is in their lives. I will always honor my mother and appreciate her gift to me of a love for the Word of God and study of the scripture. It is a great joy when my grandchildren bring to me their deep questions of theology. I love the discussions of the high school teenager who is delving into the Word. And I especially love the two, three and four-year old theology. From my platform of love for my grandchildren, the Word is spoken and their souls are formed in the likeness of Him Who came that we might have life, and have it more abundantly!

Look around you. It can be very bleak, scarey and dangerous. Then remember in Mark 4:38 the storm that was raging when the disciples panicked and said, "we're drowning!!" Jesus replied, "no, you're not! Do you see Me in this boat?" He was in the boat with them and He was not going down. Let me live knowing that Jesus is in the boat and I am safe IN THE BOAT with Him.

How do I know that with confidence? Because the Bible tells me so.

Legacy of Grace and Faith

Jeannette Clift George wrote a book called "Some Run with Feet of Clay." (George, Jeannette Clift, "Some Run with Feet of Clay," Manor of Grace, 1978) Just reading the title describes my story! "Our family does hard!" And it is hammered out on the anvil of our daily lives. Mistakes are disclosed all over our story. (Let's not go into those details here!) The lessons learned and passed on is the story of grace. My people trusted the Savior for eternal life and the forgiveness of our sins. The powerful message of faith alone in Christ alone resonates in every generation. From the great-grandmother who took her children to a little church in McComb, Mississippi, to the grandmother who was baptized in the Pearl River, to the children and grandchildren who were baptized in the Gulf of Mexico—the story is redemption. We repeat stories of challenge, world wars, the great depression, hurricanes, illnesses, and we sing the praises of God's grace that has carried us through. We invite the next generation to know the stories and the spiritual legacy behind them. We will consider later the Indian legend that says: "listen to your grandparents!"

I am blessed to have brothers and cousins who embrace this great opportunity. While we gather at the beach every summer with great fun and community, my brother Mark plans the Sunday morning worship. Around the Word he crafts a time to honor our parents and grandparents who lived in the shadow of grace. My other brother, Martin, picks up the theme and encourages two more generations to "walk worthy" and follow their lead. Both emphasize that each child and grandchild would have to make his own decision to walk this path. We are committed to the great legacy of faith!

> ***Prayer:*** May they meet Jesus Christ as their Savior and trust in Him for salvation
>
> May the Holy Spirit constantly pursue them and open their eyes. Pursue them like the hounds of Heaven.
>
> Lord, put people in their lives to give them Truth and speak into their lives (parents, teachers, church leaders, coaches, friends, family members etc).

The person who lives in God's embracing grace espouses **not** "pick yourself up by your bootstraps," but rather, "get up and fight another round." Grace means recovery. No one lives without failure. That's why we have 1 John 1:9. *"If we confess our sins, He is faithful and just to forgive us our sins and cleanse us from all unrighteousness."* That is a favorite promise of our family. We apply it to our personal lives and then we encourage each other.

The Christian way of life has been referred to as the Christian walk. *"We walk by faith, not by sight."* 2 Corinthians 5:7. *"Walk in newness of life."* Romans 6:4. Walking always involves a moment of being off balance. We as humans learn to recover from that moment until we hardly notice. Toddlers stumble until they learn to recover quickly, and before you know it, they are running. The quicker we recover, confess our sins, and resume the walk, the farther we advance in the spiritual. Just as we made mistakes and still do, so will our grandchildren. Recover! God loves you and forgives you. Tell them that!!!

Our first grandchild, Hunter, was, of course, the first to reveal to me that this idea of passing on something powerful actually worked. Yes, the other seven followed suit, but Hunter was very verbal with his announcements.

I loved it when he was in a Christian kindergarten and was learning scripture. His teacher told his mom, "I don't know who Nana is, but Hunter quotes her and says that everything in the Bible has a meaning for us." Thank you, Lord, for that answered prayer! He was not quoting Nana; He was quoting YOU.

I also loved it when he got to Middle School and then High School when a group of football players choose to get up at 6:00 a.m. before practice to go to a Bible study at church because it was the only time they had. The youth pastor and then pastor of their church met with these very engaged young men. When I got to meet Pastor Mike, I introduced myself with the message, "I have been praying for Hunter all of his life. He knows Jesus and he is very positive to His Word. I have prayed for the messenger, and sir, you are it."

Very sobering.

When I look back on the many ways a grandparent has made a difference in a life three simple yet powerful words come to mind: **pray, encourage**, **love**. Our prayers undergird the spiritual life. Encouragement is powerful. The greatest legacy we can give our loves ones is simply living the life. Some call it "walking the walk." When our grandchildren look at us may they see a life of surrender and obedience to the Lord where we use the spiritual dynamics He has given us everyday.

In a day where confusion reigns, how comforting to know that we can hold onto that power of Truth where we can speak to our grandchildren and they know they are getting absolute answers. On these principals they must then make their decisions.

Nana Camp

> ***Prayer:*** May I live my life in faithful obedience to You. May my grandchildren see my faith, my love for Jesus Christ, my obedience to Your Word, and my walk in the Power of the Holy Spirit. May they see my application of the walk clearly so they will know what to do.

Hunter's story: At dinner one evening when Hunter was a very little lad, his dad played a game while they were waiting. His directions to Hunter: you close your eyes; I am going to tell you one of your grandparent's names; when you open them, you be the grandparent and you say what they would say. Hunter got quickly involved and closed his eyes. "Now, open your eyes and be Papa." Hunter quickly looked up and said, "Hunter, be careful, don't run too fast, watch where you are going!!!" With great laughter both parents were amazed. "Now close again. Open now and become Granny." He looked up and said, "Hi, Hunter, you want some cake, cookies, sugar…." With more laughter, mom and dad tried again. "Now be Poppy." Immediately Hunter started, "hey, boys, hey, boys! You wanna look for some deer!" Complete with German accent. Rolling on the floor, Mom and Dad couldn't wait to see what would come next. "Okay, open your eyes and be Nana." Hunter lifted his head, spread his arms and said simply: "LET'S TALK ABOUT GOD.!!!" I cherish that reflection of what I impart to him—intentionally.

Family memorials are important especially on military holidays. My children's father died in a military plane crash when they were very young. His story and his sacrifice for our nation is important to us. Now, his grandchildren know his story, his airplane, his service, and his gravesite. At this place the importance of our nation and its history is passed on. Navigator wings grace his tombstone. Our grandchildren can't miss the message of "freedom through military victory," as well as the confidence of eternal life. His gravesite is a memorial.

Our daughter, Caroline, and her family had some good friends in Lubbock whose grandparents lived in the Texas hill country. During the first visit to their home she was moved by the memorial that Colonel Norris had in his living room to his years in Viet Nam as a POW at the Hanoi Hilton. While Caroline's dad had flown B-52s over Viet Nam, her friend's dad had suffered in that terrible prison. She saw his shoes, his toothbrush, the rosary he had made from fragments of metal he could find, and a picture of the cell he inhabited. This is a memorial for his grandchildren to see and learn of the sacrifice their grandfather had paid for their freedom. It was my privilege to meet Colonel and Mrs. Norris in their home and appreciate their memorial.

When we gather as a family at the beach, we have a "family dance" where we laugh, eat and "remember." It sounds rather like the festivals of the Jewish people. Always included in the tradition is the reading of the names of our family heroes. The readers are often my grandchildren who have their family names: Jackson Quint Janes after Major General John Quint Henion, Jacob Martin Janes and Garrett Martin Mathis after Lieutenant Martin Clifford Mathis, my father. This is a powerful legacy that has been passed down to them. The young ones get to know of the service of their grandfathers and great-grandfathers. They get to read their names. They are taught as we remember.

My dad fought in WWII as a 19-year-old second lieutenant. After Jerry, my first husband, died Dad and I bought season tickets to A&M football games so we could take my children and their friends. Driving home late at night he would talk to them about his service. This happened very rarely, but my children are blessed today to remember the stories Pawpaw told of the trenches. We have sons, grandsons and great-grandsons who are named Martin after him. The legacy they carry in their names is a source of great pride and valor of one who fought for their freedom and then lived a life of great honor. Such family stories are blessings that you hold. Pass them on.

The instance where a child is named after a family member, it is so special. It is important that they know about them. The mantle of blessing is priceless. My other six grandchildren have equally significant names: Joshua Dale after Lawrence Dale; Joseph Greer after Hilton Ross Greer; Hunter James after a great grandfather, James Presley; Lily Ann after her grandmother and great grandmother, Catherine Ann and Virginia Ann; Georgia Lee after both of her grandfathers, George and Jerry Lee, Genevieve Jeane after Marsha Jeanne (that's me!!).

The Power of a Life's Legacy

Jackie Green, wife of founder of the Museum of the Bible, Steve Green, and their daughter, Lauren Green McAfee, have written a beautiful book describing the different aspects of leaving a legacy. This lady has a powerful legacy to leave to her children and grandchildren. "Only One Life: How a Woman's Everyday Shapes an Eternal Legacy" (Zondervan, 2018) is a great study that I highly recommend. We have seen that "legacy is crafted by our faithful everyday choices." (p. 21). While we live out our everyday choices, we are creating a legacy for those behind us. As Mrs. Green reported in her book, I, too, am most impressed by the legacy left by Sarah Pierpont Edward, wife of the great preacher from early America, Jonathan Edwards. In 1900 their descendants included three hundred preachers, one hundred missionaries, eighty public office holders, one vice president of the United states and thirteen US senators, seventy-five military officers, thirteen college presidents, many doctors, lawyers and teachers… (p. 25) and many grandmothers.

I am reminded of the principle of standing still before Sovereign will. Nothing happens without first filtering through the Sovereign Hand of God. He knows. We can count on Him.

When God speaks to a culture that has marginalized Him, He creates a problem that cannot be solved by human means. I don't know who said that, but oh, how true it is. We see many of those examples today in hurricanes that man cannot direct or earthquakes that man cannot prevent. Our grandchildren live through such trying times. To His own He gives perfect solutions! Hallelujah!

The Word of God opens the door of clarity that the Holy Spirit might guide me through it. I pray that I am always in sync with His moving, His process. Walking with other believers especially applies to my grandchildren.

> Ps. 21:7 says, *"through the loving kindness of the Most High I will not be shaken."*

I am confident that the Sovereign God of the universe is engaged every day in my life, and in the lives of my grandchildren. God is at work! I am counting on it! My mentor reminded me that God expects only two things of me: dependence on Him and trust in Him through absolute surrender and complete obedience!

My pastor, R.B. Thieme III says often, "man is never good enough to meet God's perfect standard or bad enough to escape His Grace." I would add that God is at work in the human process. Grace is the resounding answer to our human need.

We "do hard" in our family. The solution is redemption. I once heard a pastor in Boerne say, "greatness is not made through one victory. It is hammered out on the anvil of our daily lives."

Consider the words which occur in the Bible so many times, "and so it came to pass." There is much involved in those words—the process, the details, the attacks, the people. God's plan never wavers off course. When I reach out to Him, He has already covered the distance.

Romans 8:28 is the picture of *"all things working together for good to those who love the Lord."* We can trust His Sovereignty at such a time as this. He is in the midst of His process even when we are seeing bad circumstances around us. My grandchildren face more in their culture than we ever dreamed. A crumbling culture from within is a scarey thing. I am not a "doomsday" person, but we do live in a time of crumbling morals and evil philosophies. The great barrage of prayer for them is my commitment. I have seen victories after defeats in the lives of my own children. God IS faithful and He is just. Today we have to warn elementary children about vaping drugs and sexual behavior. Really?

> ***Prayer:*** Lord, protect my eight grandchildren from the evils that surround them every day. Keep the enemy at bay and keep Your wall of fire of protection around them.

> ***Prayer:*** May my grandchildren be prepared through the Word of God to stand in "such a time as this." Strengthen them with the courage of character to resist the evil thinking of the world system and form their commitments based on obedience to You and Your Word.

A Sober Warning

> ***Prayer:*** Protect them from false teaching, for it surrounds them.

Ps. 127:3 tells us that "unless the Lord builds the house, they labor in vain who build it." Unless the Lord builds a spiritual legacy, they labor in vain who do it themselves. Psalm 129 warns, "May all who hate Zion be put to shame and turned backward. Let them be like grass upon the housetops, which withers before it grows up." There is warning to those who try to pass on to their children and grandchildren that which is not God's way, not obedient to God's Word and plan. They wither.

There is a warning to avoid teaching or passing on that which is false. Be very clear to define in your soul the message you are passing on. *"Whoever causes one of these little ones who believe in Me to stumble, it is better for him that a heavy millstone be hung around his neck, and that he be drowned in the depth of the sea."* Mt. 18:6 To lead a little one astray is frightening. It is tragic to think that one could have an influence on a child and teach him/her information that is FALSE.

I am reminded of the movie "Moana." We love to watch it with its beauty and its music. The message of the movie can be gleamed and interpreted according to your thinking. I did love the grandmother with her warm heart, beautiful swaying dance, her great capacity for the life of the ocean, her fun and joy. She draws you in. In fact, I love that cool, fun, connected-to-the-past grandmother. However, her message was not one I wanted my granddaughters to embrace. She was sure she would return as a great sea creature, a stingray, to guide her granddaughter, Moana, on her mission. Really??? Reincarnation is not something I want my girls to expect from me because it is simply not God's plan. I will never come back to them from heaven. I will wait for them as David did and said of his son's death, "*I shall go to him, but he will not return to me.*" 2 Samuel 12:23. Is this a little "picky?" Not really. Take a look at movies, shows, or books that infiltrate our children's minds. That which is false, evil or untrue is there. Teach them when the message is false. Caution is the guidepost when teaching and discerning with children the very powerful visual messages they see today.

> ***Prayer:*** Lord, protect my eight from the evils that surround them everyday. Keep the enemy at bay and keep Your wall of fire of protection around them.

There is an American Indian legend on a painting by Chris Barr called, "The Story Teller."

"The story teller weaves her tales of the ancient ones;
our yesterdays are the light of our tomorrows.
As the flute players tune, listen
to your grandparents!"
Little Feather

These American Indians of Santa Fe, New Mexico passed on the stories of their ancestors, their tribes. I wonder the content of how those stories affected the souls of the little ones. They had the power in their hands to train young ones in the way. Children, "Listen to your grandmother," and Grandmother, you answer to the Lord for what you pass on.

Know your subject. Be prepared. Know the Word of God and apply His plan. This is the way. God is not impressed if you make up stuff as you go along and is certainly not impressed if it contradicts His Word.

One more quote from Dr. Ed. Young, pastor of Second Baptist Church, Houston, TX, "come just like you are, but don't expect to stay that way." Come, grandchild, just as you are. With open arms I will welcome you and love you. Where you are walking in disobedience or sin, don't expect to stay that way!! Isn't this what Jesus did?

It is obvious that as years go by we become more and more aware that we ARE getting older and therefore, closer to "going home." In this process called "dying grace," He is still in the boat with me. I find my older grandchildren hugging me a little tighter and a little longer. I rejoice in their growing up and becoming young adults. I am excited to see their college choices and their consideration of life partners. That also means that I am aging. My hair is white; I don't run like I used to. Now, that's another book, but suffice to say that I will someday leave them. The first great comfort is that I will see them again in heaven. Once the issue of salvation is settled there is great hope for eternity and great reunions.

> ***Prayer:*** When dying grace comes to me, may they see my relationship with Jesus and surrender to Him until the very end.

> ***Prayer:*** May they be encouraged to know that eternity awaits me and them because they have believed on the Lord Jesus Christ for salvation.

The further comfort is that I have chosen a legacy which is lasting. The Word of God stands forever. *"The grass withers, the flower fades away, but the Word of our God stands forever."* Isaiah 40:8. When I am with Him in Heaven, Jesus Christ will pursue them; they are in His hands.

Until that time comes for me, I want to be as active as I can. Douglas MacArthur said, "You are as young as you think."

> ***Prayer:*** Lord, give me the "spark" of life to be vivacious and relate to the younger generation and their way of thinking.

When there is no legacy

Many dear ones have come to me and said, "I have no legacy to draw from." So many had no grandmothers that they knew or had grandmothers who were not engaged in their lives. I grieve for the loss of that precious legacy in their lives. They have to study HOW to pass on their legacy by reading (thus, the reason for the book) or watching. I have had the privilege of engaging other families in our outings and activities to model the blessing of living a legacy. We have even "adopted" some precious ones and have become their Nana and Poppy. I am grateful to the Lord for using us in this way.

At this point, I have to also give credit to my mother and my grandmother who welcomed my friends into their lives. Mother was in a wheelchair for many years, and one of the dear families we have embraced as our own took the opportunity to know her and have their children relate to a great-grandmother-figure who was handicapped. It was a sweet experience of love and grace, and Mother welcomed the opportunity to love them and speak into their lives. She just opened the door of opportunity and her heart to testify of God's perfect provision.

My basic answer to the original statement of "no legacy" is an easy one—start it! A rich spiritual foundation has to start somewhere and with someone. Bravo to those who are starting a powerful legacy that will be passed on and on and on.

Conclusion

As I look back on the many ways a grandparent has made a difference in a life three simple yet powerful words come to mind: **pray, encourage, love**. Our prayers undergird the spiritual life. Encouragement is powerful. The greatest legacy we can give our loves ones is simply living the life. Some call if "walking the walk." When our grandchildren look at us may they see a life of surrender and obedience to the Lord where we use the spiritual dynamics He has given us everyday.

In a day where confusion reigns, how comforting to know that we can hold onto that power of Truth where we can speak to our grandchildren and they know they are getting absolute answers. On these principals they must then make their decisions.

Prayer: May I live my life in faithful obedience to You.

Prayer: May my grandchildren see my faith, my love for Jesus Christ, my obedience to Your Word, and my walk in the Power of the Holy Spirit.

Prayer: May they see my application of the walk clearly so they will know what to do.

Daniel 4:3 says, "*His dominion is from generation to generation.*" Within that phrase is your story and mine. The time from one generation to the next is the story of a life lived and a story told. The vast content of that story is passed on to the next generation. We have the greatest opportunity to pass on more than just what WE think. We can pass down the great message of God's grace plan for man, and we can live out that message in faith. What greater spiritual legacy can you leave to your children—and yes, your grandchildren?

One more piece of the legacy: Keep track of the victories!!! Praise Him!!

Nana Camp

The following chapters relate a spiritual legacy through creative activities and time spent with my eight grandchildren. It answers the question, "why would they want to come to Nana's house?"

Chapter 4

Let's go to Nana's House

★ ★ ★

As these grandchildren grow, we will find reasons to engage them in our lives. I loved to go to my grandmother's house. I wanted my eight grandchildren to desire to come to my house. So, I have to ask the question: why would they want to come? My challenge was to give them a reason!

The home.

My personal perspective of the home is a place, a state of mind, and eventually, a memory. Sights, smells, sounds—can all take us back to that place. What are those senses that take you back to your home in your memory?

The primary setting for your grandparent-grandchild adventure is, of course, the home. In her book, *Radical Womanhood—Feminine Faith in a Feminist World*, (McCulley, Carolyn, Moody Publishers, 1963, p.94) Carolyn McCulley discusses the value of the home base. She states that "*the history of domesticity is relevant to the ongoing feminist discussion about where women should invest their time and energy…the golden age of domesticity, the real roots of home economics, and how consumer marketing has shaped much of our culture's assessment of the home. Nevertheless, Scripture is very clear that wisdom or folly is demonstrated by how a woman treats her home. 'The wise woman builds her house, but with her own hands the foolish one tears hers down.'* Proverbs 14:1 NIV)."

Of course, in our discussion, we must note that a grandparent's home is different than the one the parent grew up in. Welcoming our children back home is not the same as welcoming our grandchildren into our homes. We are not trying to create that place where he grows, learns, is disciplined, and is formed into the adult he is to be. Our focus is on that safe place where we can minister one-step-removed from this mission of raising children to the "task" of encouraging our grandchildren. I never want to imply that our job is "raising." It is "nurturing." There is a big difference.

The author and poet laureate, Natasha Tretheway, says, "The power of place is that it connects us to our pasts and, often, to our dreams of the future. The places we've known hold within them traces of our emotional geography, and inner landscape, associated with particular moments of our lives… going back to New Orleans to visit my father… connected me to the days of my early childhood, the happy triptych (three hinged pictures) of mother, father, and child set against a backdrop of lush flora, of architectural beauty, the musicality of language and the pleasure of books." (Trethewey, "Southern Living," Nov. 2018, p. 70–71) All of this is connected to a place.

Paula Disbrowe describes a grand family reunion at her family's farm. (Disbrowe, Paula, "Southern Living," November, 2018, p. 59–64) "Every November, a grandmother's legacy calls a family back to its historic south Carolina homestead for a feast of food and memories." This makes me smile. Dennis Power had been given his grandmother's cast iron pan and her butcher knife… and had cherished them for 40 years. "The moment the skillet slipped through his fingers and cracked on the brick steps, everything changed. 'It was like it cracked that literal connection to her hands, her cooking, and the place we came from.'" (Ibid) This speaks to the power of the place and the "things" that represent that very special person, Grandmother.

"Though they might disagree about who makes the best nut cake, they're convinced that this annual gathering helps maintain their connection.' Mama was a peacemaker and taught us that nothing was worth an argument,' says Aunt Dot with a laugh." (Ibid) This mamma/grandmother accomplished a wonderful phenomenon, a traditional gathering and a message, especially the message.

> ***Prayer:*** Lord, let my children remember **something** that I say.

Ask any of my children what Grandma Odia used to say, and they will reply, "ain't nothing going to happen today that me and the Lord can't handle." You will also find this hanging in some of their homes.

Carolyn McCully discusses the change in the concept of the home through the decades. *"All the comfort of home' took on a new meaning in the last few decades. Home wasn't always such a collection of creature comforts, though. In fact, for most of recorded history, the bulk of humanity lived in simple dwellings. Except for the wealthy and the ruling class, most everyone's homes in antiquity were utilitarian, rather than monuments to personal style and taste."* (McCulley, Carolyn, "Radical Womanhood," Moody Publishers, Chicago, Ill. 2008, p. 99). She continues to note that Abraham and Sarah's home was a tent. Homes of antiquity did not have windows, but simple rooms that opened onto a courtyard. Furniture was simple with the inhabitants sleeping on a bedroll.

By the time the Hebrews settled in Canaan their homes expanded to four-room dwellings with tramped-down earth floors and rooms for animals. *"The home may not have been a place of luxury, but it was a place of community... women were largely responsible for caring for the children and making clothing and food....*" (Ibid, p. 94) The community of women was close, binding, and often necessary for survival. I can imagine the communication as the ladies met at the well, pounded bread, or wove their fabrics. Children learned valuable lessons from just listening to the mother, aunt, or grandmother tell the lessons of life and stories of the family. Today it is with planned intention that ladies gather, and it takes a greater effort to include the young ones.

It is my joy to hear of "girl time," gatherings where females of the family get together. These are the opportunities to have more than just a fun time. They are opportunities to pass on your family values to the next generation. Who else is going to tell the stories of the past? Can't you imagine Sarah's stories at the well or her reaction when Abraham said, "Pack our things we are following God to an unknown place to raise the children." (What children???) Surely she shared this dilemma with the women in her life.

Now inject into this ancient setting the grandmother who had ample opportunity to be an integral part of the lives of her grandchildren. Community was the routine of life, and her wisdom was greatly valued.

Through the decades the profile of the home has changed from the place where mom orchestrated its life to the place where career mom comes and goes from homemaker to career woman. Still, the basic institution of society is the home. As goes the family unit, so goes the nation. William Ross Wallace wrote a poem in about 1865 that states, "The hand that rocks the cradle rules the world."

Visiting Grandmother's house can still be rich with these "legacy lessons" whether experienced in the daily routine of life or with intent and planned concentration. Wouldn't you love to know this grandmother as Amy Peterman describes her? "My grandma taught me all kinds of things just by my being around her when I was younger. She loved gardening, crocheting, baking, and sewing. She always had beautifully polished nails even though she worked in the garden. She wore lovely lace-topped nightgowns and she smelled so sweet. But best of all, she always said to me, 'bless your heart'." ("Grandmothers," p. 39)

Coming to Nana and Poppy's house and then sitting down and watching TV (which we do enjoy!) is not the best use of the time we are given. Creating space and time and activities is what has worked for us. I really loved it when our grandchildren would come from out of town to visit. They would race into the house, give us a quick hug, and then go to find the toys, rooms, areas where they had last left their treasures at Nana and Poppy's house. And there they were, ready for the small hands to embrace them again. Our grandchildren always feel welcome and comfortable when they come to visit.

My granddaughters, Georgia and Genny, can invite visitors in and escort them to the areas with which they are very familiar. They can get the dishes and silverware and set the table without any help from me. They have been here before, and they are comfortable! When giving them inviting reasons to come, I always love to spring surprises—things that are new or different. For example, the American girl dolls upstairs that they left dressed for a beach adventure might now be found dressed for a proper tea. I love to catch them off guard, and they are delighted. It's part of the fun and ambiance of coming to Nana's house!

Carolyn McCulley observes in her book, "*Radical Womanhood*," (McCulley, Carolyn, "*Radical Womanhood*," Moody Publishers, Chicago, Ill, 2008) two examples of the blessing of the home.

> *"God settles the solitary in a home; he leads out the prisoners to prosperity but the rebellious dwell in a parched land."* PSALM 68:6

> *"He gives the barren woman a home, making her the joyous mother of children. Praise the Lord."* PSALM 113:9

"One way God chooses to bless people is by providing a home—a haven in a harsh world and a place where relationships can thrive and be fruitful.... Paul instructs

Christian women not to neglect their homes. Titus 2:3–5 says, *"Older women, likewise, are to be reverent in behavior, not slanderers or slaves to much wine. They are to teach what is good, and so train the young women to love their husbands and children, to be self-controlled, pure, working at home, kind and submissive to their own husbands, that the Word of God may not be reviled."* (Ibid)

Now there is a format for a Godly home where a grandmother abides. She has raised her own children, and now opens her door and her heart to her grandchildren.

> ***Prayer:*** Lord, use my home for your glory. Let it be a place where I represent You and the path of life. May my grandchildren see and learn how to love and honor you.

McCulley continues, "Every sphere has its repetitive tasks that contribute to the larger goal of productivity. The point of being a keeper at home is to provide a haven for a godly family to thrive… to offer hospitality to fellow Christians and non-Christians alike, and to provide a place for the church to meet…. Hospitality remains a command for all believers throughout the ages; *"contribute to the needs of the saints and seek to show hospitality."* Romans 12:13 (Ibid)

> ***Prayer:*** Make my home a comfortable, inviting place where they come and know that Jesus abides here.

A prayer group has met at my home for over 30 years. When Georgia was a baby, I kept her several days a week. She was in my home during the gathering of ladies. When she was tiny, she just slept or rested in my arms. Then as she crawled, we welcomed her to be among us. As she toddled, I gave her a pencil to mimic our notes as we added to our prayer lists. Then she began to write on each ladies list and apply stickers. Those prayer partners did not want her to stop. They cherish those old prayer lists with Georgia's additions on them. She was welcomed into the community of women, especially those who pray. It is an indelible part of her soul. Then her sister, Genny, came along and did the same thing. I grew to welcome them as part of our prayer group. Both girls were raised in the community of women who pray.

History repeats itself. Grandmother had taken me to her Sunday School class where I was surrounded by women who prayed and studied the Word under her. I still feel the strong presence of women, including Mother and Aunt Mary, who walked with the Lord and embraced me in their midst. This creates a legacy, generation after generation, that is rooted in the Lord Himself and His Word.

The study of the makeup of the home and the impact of the industrial revolution which took the emphasis of society away from the home is a fascinating one. It explains the world in which our grandchildren are growing up. We cannot turn back the clock, though some families try, but we can seek to understand the culture and how it impacts our children.

Again, Carolyn McCulley explains the attacks made on the home, the "stay-at-home," mom and the politics surrounding them. She concludes that "the heart of the home is found in the relationships nurtured there and the comfort offered to one another." (p. 115). The picture of a peaceful, inviting home is so powerful that the Lord uses it Himself when He states that *"in My Father's house are many mansions."* John 14:1–3. "He did not leave us to prepare another cubicle in His Father's office—thank God!" (Ibid). He promises a warm, inviting, eternal haven, an eternal home.

Bedtime routine.

Can you close your eyes and still remember the peace, the incredible stillness of nestling down in a bed and feeling secure? It can be in a big, down-filled, luxury bed, a sofa made into a bed, or a pallet on the floor. The logistics matter little, but the place is all-important. The day ends and Grandmother is tucking you in. I love it when I put my little ones, and now not so little ones, to bed. They still let me say prayers, rub their backs, and always sing a special song. These are the most precious times of conversation and sharing thoughts and secrets.

Christopher De Vinck remembers "the hand of my grandmother. She would bring her hand down in the darkness as she stood over my bed before I slept. I was ten. She was eighty. She'd place her hand on my head and offer a blessings in Flemish: 'a cross and a sleep well', she'd whisper." (Grandmothers, p. 30)

When my grandchildren were young, we would always tell a story. Instead of a tale known to them, I would make up elaborate stories.

Make up your stories! Some grandparents are just natural story tellers. I had this great experience with my daughter's boys. I would put them to bed and take time to tell stories. The same stories just got more and more involved until they were unforgettable adventures.

I would tell the adventures of going to grandmother and grandfather's house. I did not use names so they could put themselves into the story. When they were very young, they would delight in figuring out which character they were. As I spoke of the oldest boy, the middle boy, and the little boy, they would smile at each other. When I spoke of the strong, red-headed, curly haired boy, Jacob would say, "that's me!" When I spoke of the oldest boy who would look after the rest, Jackson would say, "that's me!"

Once upon a time there were three little boys who went to visit Grandmother and Grandfather. There was a big boy, the middle boy, and the blonde boy. They packed their suitcases and traveled far to Grandmother's. They played hard all day. That night they unpacked their suitcase and toothbrushes, and got ready for bed. All three boys slept upstairs in the large four-poster bed. The big boy and the middle boy on the sides, and the blonde boy in the middle. Grandfather brought them popcorn for a snack to eat in bed—now that's a treat! The weather turned cold and windy, so Grandmother got lots of blankets as they settled in and snuggled close to each other. Grandmother heard their prayers, tucked them in, and turned out the light.

The blonde boy was safe in the middle, but just the same, he looked at the other two boys for comfort. They were almost asleep when they heard a scratch coming from somewhere (here is when you make the sound!!). When they heard it again the blonde boy said, "what is THAT?" The other two boys sat up and said, "it's ok, we are very brave." It was coming from outside the window. Instead of calling for Grandfather as the blonde boy suggested, the older boy decided to just peek out the window. He got up on his knees and held on to the poster. The second boy followed him as the blonde boy burrowed farther under the covers.

The two boys looked at each other with big eyes, parted the curtains, and opened the blinds. Two large white eyes were looking back at them. "Whoooooo? Whoooo? Whoooo are you?" it cried. The large hoot owl was sitting on the branch of the large tree next to the house.

"We are here visiting our grandparents! Who are you??" they answered. The owl was as frightened as they were and flew away into the neighbor's tree.

Disaster averted, they settled back into bed to assure the blonde boy that all was well.

Now, my story goes on and on, and it certainly grew as the years passed. It even included a "bullagator" under the bed. I am sure there are many imaginary stories in you, just waiting to be told.

Then there are the great stories of their family members from the past. They loved to hear the war stories of their great grandfather, stories of their great great grandmother during the depression. Especially delightful are the stories you tell them of their parents. I love to tell the story and then say, "do you know who that was?" Of course, there are some stories better left untold. These are great pieces of the puzzle of the legacy that has been left to them to discover.

And don't forget the great story of when they were born. Now, that's a treasure for each one. Mine love to hear the people who were just waiting for them, the treasure God had created.

"I will give thanks to Thee, for I am fearfully and wonderfully make… my frame was not hidden from Thee, when I was made in secret." PSALM 139:14–15

Read, tell stories, sing, and peace falls upon the room as eyes close.

Songs

We love to sing, and we don't have many great voices. The one exception is Josh!! We're so grateful for Josh!

My grandmother could not carry a tune, but I remember to this day the old spirituals she would sing. My favorite is one of the songs we call "Grandma Odia songs."

Nana Camp

Blessed Assurance, Jesus is mine.
Oh, what a foretaste of glory divine.
Heir of salvation, purchase of God,
Born of His spirit, washed in His blood.
This is my story! This is my song!
Praising my Savior all the day long.
This is my story! This is my song.
Praising my Savior all the day long. (FANNY CROSBY)

We sing that loudly. Wherever it is sung, each of my grandchildren gets a special smile of his face as he or she begins to sing. I know they are thinking of Nana, just like I am thinking of Odia.

The verses go on with a great message of doctrine, hope, and Jesus. Songs are great platforms to teach reiterate the Truth of Scripture and anchor it in our souls.

Very early in my journey as Nana, I began to add verses to that song. With each new grandchild I added a verse. After 20 years, this is now my contribution:

Eight little children. *Seven days of fun.*
Six moms and dads, *five boys on the run.*
Four very fine Janes boys. *Four Griffiths too.*
Three little girls, *grandparents two by two.*
This is my story, this is my song! *Praising my Savior all the day long.*

Find a song. There should be a message in that song that you want them to remember, but the song itself is a connection between the two of you. Sing it over and over. Sing it at bedtime; sing it in the car, etc. They will soon be singing it with you and even when you are not there.

My song: "Blessed Assurance, Jesus is Mine."

Hunter and his mom: "My Girl"

Georgia with her daddy: "You are my sunshine"

My Mom: "Getting to Know you"

A friend emailed me once to tell me the song she had chosen for her new grandchild. She had heard my stories and her song was unique to her!

My grandmother sang to me. Among others, she loved "When They Ring Those Golden Bells."

> *Prayer:* give me a unique connection with each child.

> *Prayer:* give them a reason to come

Simple Fun

It has been a blessing to me to hear young people speak of their grandmothers. The young man who is my oldest grandson's roommate who spoke of the grandmother's cookie jar that was always filled. (I don't even have a cookie jar!).

People have often asked what I do with my grandchildren. The following are a few examples which are pretty simple, and you won't need a helicopter or a big budget:

- **Ride bikes**. And that means you have to get on one. Poppy and I make sure they have one their size. We start around the block and expand. Every Christmas my oldest and I rode the "midnight ride"—well, not really midnight. We judged the "best Christmas house" in the neighborhood. When Hunter was 14 we were still doing that. Then, the next in line, Jackson, and I did the same.
- **Skate, ski**. Whatever is fun for them is worth your consideration. Now, these are not options for me. I have a limit to "adventures" that involve speed. No roller coasters! But I do try new things. I must admit here that my grandmother was NOT an adventurer. She never rode a bike; did not swim; never drove a car, and none of that mattered to her grandchildren. So, rest easy, you grandmothers who do not care for adventure! It's not required.

- **Read**. That's easy. Just get good books.
- **Dress up.** I have a chest upstairs for them to explore at my house. I let them create and then take their pictures. They love it, and now they are treasures. I had to encourage them when they were toddlers, but after a few years they needed no encouragement! Now the older ones teach the youngest grandchildren how to dress up and use their imaginations.

I had a dear friend share the idea of a "fashion show" where she narrated their creations. I loved the idea and we had a ball! We invited friends one year to join the adventure and creativity!!!

- **Tea party.** This can be done with fancy dress from the chest with hats, of course. One day Georgia and I got out all the stuffed animals. She dressed up the stuffed bears and sang. She loved it and then Lily wanted to do the same. And then there was the joy of a two-year-old tea party with a friend's granddaughter. That was classic! And, of course, there's the adventure of sitting grandfather down to tea. Poppy was a quick learner with Genny.

Every grandmother has her own unique way of relating to her grandchildren. I loved it when my friend, Camille, wrote to me about her time with her grandchildren: "my two young ones came for the last two days to write poetry, listen to classical music, play chess and swim! I am exhausted but in a good way... they listened so well. Carolina and Eva loved my French omlettes. We prayed a bit and enjoyed two movies, ate at the Avalon Diner and met my neighbors. They read their poetry and performed piano music for my neighbor and I was so proud of them!" This is such a cultured grandmother who is giving much to her grandchildren. She is, by the way, a concert pianist. I need to learn from her example!

- **Obstacle courses** in the garage with dominoes and small cars. Finding small hidden objects in a box of beans or rice, such as a bulldozer, dump truck
- **Card games** such as Go Fish, Slap Jack, Kings in the Corner, Gin rummy.
- **Board games**, jig saw puzzles, hide and find objects. We have found an engaging activity at the beach where we create our own puzzle. There are companies who make these puzzles. Each person in the family draws part of the puzzle. They especially love to put themselves into the picture doing their favorite thing at the family vacation.
- **Pictionery**, coloring together.
- **Feeding the birds** with grandfather. Our tradition is established by Poppy. It is a tradition in our home for each child to spread the birdseed, go inside, and wait at the window for the birds to come. So simple and so special.

The benefit of doing simple activities together has no boundaries and doesn't require a check book.

Holidays

Holidays are great times to establish traditions. I'm sure you could write a book on the family holiday traditions that define your family. Ours are numerous.

As my grandchildren came we established the tradition of worshipping all together on Christmas Eve. We could do this at First Baptist Church, Houston. Did I mention that my two little granddaughters are the sixth generation, yes **sixth**, that have been members there. My great grandmother started this line. Yes, that's another book!

As we worshipped and listed to Pastor Gregg Matte tell the story of Luke 2, he explained that "life can be a bumpy ride," especially if you are on a donkey on the road to Bethlehem. He encouraged us that when many will say, "no room," it creates an air of uneasiness and fear. We can only imagine how Mary and Joseph felt. There is comfort in the familiar. When we are out of our comfort zone and far from the familiar, as these two were with a baby ready to deliver, a town with no place to welcome them, no midwife, and the knowledge of this unique baby. All unfamiliar territory. And then He shows up and we remember that in His Name is our home. What did the pastor mean by that? My take-away was that our security, no matter what the circumstances, rests in the Name, or the character, of the eternal God. When I know Him and the security that comes from Who and What He is, I can rest. And in the story, then came Jesus! Pastor Matte noted what God had done to get Mary and Joseph where they were when "it came to pass." I looked at all sixteen of my children and grandchildren gathered to worship and considered what God had done to get us there. Then I looked forward to what He had planned for the future, rejoicing in the anticipation of something new. Wow! I could not imagine what the next chapters would unfold.

Travel

Travel is a wonderful gift you can give your grandchildren. Of course, not all of us can engage in grand travel. If you can, there is a resource that you can research at www.roadscholar.org. It has an agenda especially planned for grandparents and grandchildren. It looks like a great adventure.

I heard of seventeen (yes, seventeen) grandchildren who gathered for camp with matching t-shirts. I know grandparents who take their grandchildren to Europe, on cruises, or Camp Pops that flew grandchildren over Mount Rushmore in a helicopter.

One of my great memories is of the year my son, T.J, and I took my three granddaughters (then 14, 10, and 6) to Callaway Gardens, Georgia. Two were his daughters. While he took the two older girls on the zip lines in the trees, I took Genny (then 6) on a tandem bike ride. Now, that meant that I was in charge of the journey around the lake (at 72) and had to keep that bicycle moving and upright! It was a challenge for me and an adventure for her—a little scarey at first as I balanced to keep us upright, but off we went. I told her to peddle hard to help me—and she did! It was exhausting. I was dripping with sweat (and Southern ladies don't sweat!). It was one of my greatest memories with that six-year-old granddaughter and worth every effort of strength. Thank you, Lord, for keeping us upright. This was a stretch for me.

So, I would encourage you to try new things and stretch yourself. It will be worth the adventure.

I started a tradition with our oldest grandson, Hunter, that involved a trip at the end of his senior year in high school. Because he had the foundation of Nana Camp and some great trips, this invitation was not a big surprise. It is important to set guidelines, mine being any city in the continental United States and the opportunity to invite one person. He had never been to Washington, D.C. so it was easy to settle on that choice. The surprise was that he invited his dad, my son. We had the most wonderful four days in the nation's capitol, had great fun, and enjoyed the memorable monuments and memorials.

As this writing adventure approaches the end, our second grandson, Jackson, has graduated from high school and navigated through the COVID-19 challenges. The city he chose was New York, and his traveling companion, his dad, Jason. We began to plan our visits to Broadway when New York became the COVID epicenter. Our trip has been cancelled, he has graduated, and Jason and I are trying to plan a safe, outdoor, social-distancing trip to the Grand Canyon. He has decided that it will be a great adventure to fly over that national treasure.

Each grandchild will choose a different format. Each trip a different celebration for them, and especially for me!

When I invited my brother's two granddaughters, Lila and Cora, to be the last in a long line of Nana Campers, Georgia Lee explained to them just what Nana Camp was. It was the cutest presentation, but I loved when she said, "and when you graduate high school, she will take you anywhere you want to go." Not quite!

Our annual destination vacation is the beach. This is an example of a family vacation which includes traditions they will remember and anticipate every year. The activities we have done for years become part of the adventure. In 2020, I have been part of five generations that have loved the beach vacation. One generation prepares the way for the next to enjoy the same adventures. It's no wonder the beach is my favorite place to get away.

Our traditions become a platform for that opportunity to represent the Lord Jesus and lessons from His Word. Oh, the Truths that have been passed on in such a fun environment. That platform includes a place to speak and be heard, to offer divine solutions, and to just "talk." So much has been resolved in those front porch visits or those long, lazy days in the sun, or those peaceful gatherings by the pool. Oh, and then there's the ride in the four-wheeler with just the grandchild and Poppy. You can't beat that.

Each year my family would rent houses at Galveston, Texas. Generations would pile into two houses and the adventures would begin. In 1999 we moved our location to Mustang Island, down the coast. Old traditions continued and gave way to new adventures.

- ★ **Sandcastles** are a must at the beach. One year I hired a gentleman to teach us how to correctly construct the sandcastle. They still remember, "plop, scoop, jiggle."
- ★ **Surfing** lessons from Uncle T. J. Our youngest son is father to two and uncle to six. He and his wife, Emily, are excellent surfers (left over from their younger days). As each child became of age, Uncle T. would give them surfing lessons. When the surf is up we have some accomplished surfers.

- **Fishing**.
- **Shells**, shells, shells, and all the crafts one can make.
- **Long walks**.
- **Fires**.
- The infamous **scavenger hunt**, where each team has the same lists of senerios to capture on a cell phone is always a favorite. When competing against my two brothers' or cousins' teams, my team usually won. Items included: kiss a grandfather, "Tim Tebow" on the beach, handstand on the beach, hug a cousin, leap frog, pledge allegiance to the flag, the Mathis girls, the Griffith girls, dance with an uncle, and so it goes. Great adventure!
- **Puzzle** with a blank canvas where everyone draws themselves into the picture. We have quite a collection which provides great memories. Then, of course, there is the regular puzzle to put together as a group.
- **Family dance** is a special memory. The gathering centered around a meal with a dance where everyone was invited to participate. Grandmother danced with grandson. The new baby danced with Mom or Dad. Cousins danced with each other. We even had a great DJ in "Uncle Chuck," who honored people and events through his microphone. The person who had turned 50 was usually roasted. The newly engaged couple danced a special dance.

Our military veterans were honored as their names were read and little ones marched around to "It's a Grand 'Ole Flag." Special memories became even more significant.

No limits

Nana Camp (coming up in the next chapter) is only the beginning. There are no limits to the fun I have with my grandchildren! I can turn a funeral service into an adventure.

Of course, we had the soloist at my mother's funeral service sing the song that she and my grandmother had sung to all of us, "Blessed Assurance, Jesus is mine." As the singer began, it took my grandchildren a few moments to recognize this special song. Then they looked at each other with big eyes, and acknowledged, "that is our Grandma Odia song" And slowly they began to sing with him. By the time he got it: "this is my story, this is my song..." they were all singing and the congregation had joined in with them.

While driving to the grave site, my daughter and one daughter-in-law had a few of the children in the car, and the conversation went like this: Hunter (the cool teenager): "you know, we are driving through a bunch of dead bodies." Jacob (5 years), looking at all the grave markers, "I think Jesus died somewhere around here."

Lily (knowledgeable 6 years), "He did not! He died in London!" We still laugh about their candor.

For Mom's funeral we had a friend in charge of each of the little ones. My friend, Theresa, held Joe's hand as we approached the graveside service with the casket settled in the right place. He asked her, "so, what's in the treasure box?" She answered, "a treasure." Mom's service was a great time for answering questions from her great grandchildren. Their parents and their grandparents took the opportunity and increased their understanding of death and life everlasting.

I cherish the memory of a conversation I had with Joshua (then 8 years old) the next morning. He asked me to come outside with him in our tea garden in the front yard. After a chatty conversation, I said, "Josh, what's on your mind?" He explained to me that he knew Nanny was in heaven-home, and since that was true, what was in the "box?" And did we bury her in the ground. Great question! We had a great eight-year-old theology discussion about the body, soul, and spirit, the rapture of the body, and resurrection. He was satisfied and had great comfort in what would happen to him someday.

Their life and time with you become the rhythm of repetition and opportunity.

There are no limits to what your imagination can come up with! It's a great adventure, for the grandchildren and for you! And their parents will be very impressed.

Some fun things we have done

- **Bed time traditions**. We read, sing the same songs, and tell stories.
- **Gathering** ALL the grandchildren. Wherever this is, it is a sweet time together (now from 21 to age 6). They still figure out how to relate to each other.
- **Ride the bus** to town. I have been doing this since I was a little girl. My dad was a bank vice-president in downtown Houston. It was the tradition that my children still remember, to meet him at James Coney Island at Christmas, go to his office (wow), see the Christmas trees in the windows, eat Gingerbread and drink wassail in the lobby of Bank of the Southwest (a long-gone tradition), and hear the choir at Texas Commerce Bank (also in the past). My first grandchildren got to participate, but that is gone for the younger ones. They get to ice skate instead!
- Don't miss the **rodeo**! It's a great Texas tradition.
- **Go to the park**, any park, zoo, or museum. Your city will hold unique attractions, and the repetition of these visits create a rhythm of fun and memories.
- Play a **ball game** with them. Getting the entire family involved is fabulous if you can make that happen. Going to the park or playing on a real diamond adds great value to the day.

- ★ **Cook** with them. Most grandmothers do this better than I, but we have a great time.
- ★ **Crafts,** anything you can think of! And then they will be teaching you.
- ★ **Write, draw** and send their work to other family members.

Every single time you are with them!!!!

Every single time you are with them is a rich blessing, better known in Scripture as "redeeming the time" with your grandchildren.

Now, let's go to Nana Camp.

Chapter 5

Nana Camp 101 (no parents, please)

★ ★ ★

Nana Camp began for me in 2003. My best friend, Jane, and I engaged our two grandsons (Hunter who was 4 and Maric who was 5) in a planned adventure. I know there are many forms of this special time. I first heard of "Camp Grammy" in passing from a friend. It planted the seed and captured my interest. Some grandparents do this together (camp Noni/Grandpa). Some grandfathers, such as my friend and dermatologist, take the lead (Camp Pops). I love the many forms. This is my story.

My definition of "Nana Camp" is:

a time, a place, an intentional commitment to be executed by a grandmother with her grandchildren.

It has been defined and developed over the years and has required careful organization. **Nana Camp is the designated time set aside for grandchildren who are the participants. It is dedicated to playing, teaching**

and engaging the children. Nana Camp is a great field trip, a giant slumber party, the presentation of theology for children that goes on and on for days. It builds community among the leaders and the campers. Most of all, it is great fun.

Planning is imperative. Some of the required necessities:

- **Notebooks**. These become very personal. They include worksheets, prayer lists, pictures of what they are learning, etc. Worksheets are any papers they work on during camp. They include puzzles, fill-in-the-blanks, diagrams, coloring pages. These can get as intricate as you wish. They should always be age-appropriate. Some grandmothers have their grandchildren keep a diary of each day. I could never get this going, but it's a great idea. As in school, they decorate these notebooks with great creativity. They can get them out at home and review with their parents what they learned.
- **Backpacks or bags**. As we gather special items and treasures during the week, the campers keep them in their backpacks. Of course, these have been personalized and decorated.
- **Flashlights**. big surprise for those night-time activities
- **Pens**. Each child gets his/her own set of new markers each year.

Nana Camp

- **Drawing pads.**
- **Their special pillows** or "luvies" brought from home.
- ★ WHATEVER ELSE YOU NEED TO ENGAGE THEM.
- **Make a schedule.** You probably won't be able to do everything you plan. We never do! Make sure there is plenty of fun which includes activities that they will really enjoy.

We stay so busy and engaged that they hardly have time to get into trouble. Mine often ask for "free time" when they can choose whatever they want to do. I laughed the first time they asked, and I realized that I had to build in time for them just to be together. Nana also learns at Nana Camp. Now my niece helps me make "lesson plans!"

Traditions

- **Welcome.** The first-year campers are brought into the group with some sort of "welcome." We have done crazy string, run through a hands-up-made tunnel, high-fives, and so on. Your imagination will create wonderful tradition.
- **A pillow case** is made for the new camper with everyone's signature on it.
- **Build-a-bear.** This involves a trip to the store where everyone helps the new camper pick out his bear and dress it. It's very sweet to watch all of

the suggestions from brothers/sisters/cousins. They can bring their bear every year. We have chosen bears in camouflage for the boys, bears in athletic uniforms, my little ponies, frilly cupcake bears, lions, and even bunnies. It's a personal choice and so much fun!

Activities

- **Make a plate** ("Makit"™). Each child has his own plate, and I have a collection! This creates a great memory. Incorporate the theme and it becomes a reminder of what was learned.
- **Shopping.** When we explore and visit gift shops we collect treasures and memories from the places we have been. The rule: *pick out ONE thing*. This often involves a big decision. We have collected rocks, bows and arrows, marble turtles, walking sticks, scorpions in a paper weight, every manner of stuffed animal, coon skin caps, beautiful jewelry, and on and on.
- **Pictures.** They speak volumes and become personal treasures that are brought out for years to come. Pictures they draw are their sources of pride of accomplishment in production and expression, and become your remembrances. These pictures will record memories with their own work. Display it!

- **Frame the pictures** they draw! What an honor to have your art hanging in Nana's home. I have seen many homes decorated with children's art. Evie Sue, my son's mother-in-law, has dedicated a wall in her home to the art of her grandchildren. Very cool! It can be stuck on the wall or framed in beautiful frames. So creative!
- **Pictures books** become a history of your traditions. Some still use the old "scrapbook" method where pictures are secured in a book. I make a picture book (Shutterfly ™ is my preference.) for each family of the camp pictures. It is a documentary of the legacy carrying on.

I love to see grandchildren's photos or portraits displayed in homes, whether subtle or grand. There is a special honor associated with them. I have multiple pictures of myself with each grandchild hanging in my gallery. It shows them growing up as unique individuals to their Nana, and what a day when Hunter passed me in height—caught in his pictures on the wall! I have their current pictures in a bookcase, their one-year-old and two-year-old photos in my hall, and now the second high school senior picture ready to hang. These are milestones in their lives and I love to honor them.

- **Art.** Remember those drawing pads from the supply list? If a trip is involved, draw in the car! One focus is to draw what you see. Another is to draw what you hear. I play children's music on CDs. This requires a little planning to get the CDs ready to play in the car. Today it is thumb drives, but still takes a little planning. They listen to the songs (hopefully story songs) and draw what they hear. Then in the evening we look at their pictures and guess the songs that we have all heard. I end up photographing pictures to include in the memory book. The older ones still remember those songs and can sing them with the young campers.

★ **Flags.** They make their own and it is fun, creative, and very personal. The concept is from Song of Solomon 2:4 *"Your banner over me is love."* We live our lives under the banner of God's plan and His unique call on each of us. He made us a certain way and He gives us gifts. So, this project involves several steps:

(1) supplies include a dowel stick, fabric to create the flag/banner, paint or pens to draw.

(2) Exercise of having the one who knows you the best (brother, sister, aunt) describe you in one word. We have heard "she loves me," "she is a good sister," "she likes to read."

(3) Describe yourself. (I am _____, I like to _____)

(4) draw those things and whatever else you want on your banner.
(5) describe your banner.
(6) go outside and "fly it."

I love to see what they come up with. We have had such things as: Jesus, the cross, art, books, sports (soccer, volleyball), happy face, group of friends, etc.

- **Finger puppets.** They can be purchased or made. The children create their own stories, OR Nana tells the story and they act out with the puppets on their fingers.
- **Finger paint.** Now, who doesn't love to finger paint. Give them a topic or just let them go.
- **Slime.** Enough said.
- **Note cards.** These can be purchased or created. One year Nana purchased a set for each camper with artwork that Georgia had created and printed on cards. They can write home, to family or friends (which means you have to mail them) or to each other. We have written to our hostess, to our teenage counsellor, to each other. These are especially meaningful, especially if there have been moments of conflict (oh, yes!!!) and someone wants to reach out or bridge a gap. I am always amazed at the heart of these young ones. How good is God to put them in this arena and teach them the art of love and

forgiveness—often in a notecard. The first time I saw this happen I shouted "hallelujah" in my soul.

- **Notes from parents.** They are read during camp and are always precious. Of course, this requires the planning of soliciting the notes from the parents beforehand. We usually do not have the issue of anyone being homesick, so this is always fun.
- **Spa Time** is a sweet way to appreciate Nana and the helpers with foot massage, hand massage, warm towels. Of course, they need a little help with this, but it is one of my girls' favorite things. Painting nails is a must.

    It's also fun to go to the nail salon. Memow, my best friend who has become a special part of Nana Camp, started this tradition and we ended up with more colors and designs. The girls were tickled with Nana and Memow's colored toes!
- **Puzzles.** Solving them is an inclusive activity where all cooperate. I try to find puzzles that support the theme of Nana Camp. Then there's the community puzzles that are blank canvases on which to draw and create their collective stories. How much fun for each person to draw onto that blank puzzle, meaning they design their own.

Suggested songs:
- ★ "Jesus Loves Me"
- ★ "Texas, Our Texas"
- ★ "God Bless America"
- ★ "The Star Spangled Banner"
- ★ "Be Ye Kind" (tune of "three blind mice")

  Be ye kind, one to another, tenderhearted, forgiving one another.
  Even as God for Christ sake has forgiven you.
  Ephesians 4:32… oh, be ye kind

  There are so many memories connected to this song. Cora singing it softly as we walked along at Natural Bridge Caverns. Georgia singing it in an elevator at Sea World when someone had been sassy to her. (Not sure it was appropriate at the moment, but it spoke to the issue)

- ★ "On the Road again" by Willie Nelson

  This is always first song we listen to in the car when traveling. They sing with gusto and slap hands at the part that says, "we are the best of friends."

Themes of Nana Camp

Over the years when asked what I was doing for Nana Camp each year, I would share the "theme" and the activities that supported that theme. As more friends asked, I began to keep a record. These are mine. I would love to hear yours!

Prayer is always involved in choosing the theme. Like any other venture, prayer seeks the Lord's will and sets the stage for His agenda. As the years passed my "campers" would suggest themes to be explored the next year. I loved when Lily said, "Let's do sea creatures. And the Bible story can be Jonah and the whale." She set the theme for the next year.

The idea is the umbrella under which we explore. It keeps their attention and motivates their interest. The theme ties it all together visually and defines the learning.

Every year Nana Camp takes on a life of its own. It can often spin out of control with motivated campers adding new topics, projects, and adventures. It's fun to pursue these side trips for a time, but often Nana has to pull it back together to refocus on the objective. I find that the overriding theme can be used to put everything back into focus. Any good teacher will agree that enthusiasm is a desired result, but can often become a distraction.

The themes of Nana Camp have been fun, educational, and beneficial for me and for my grandchildren.

Texas

This is a general introduction to learn about Texas and has been repeated over several years.

Activities:
- Define city, **state** and nation.
- Color the **shape** of the state on a worksheet.
- Identify the **Texas flag**.
- Teach the **history** of the state. There are great vast resources to be discovered.
- Identify **heroes of Texas**. This turns into a great character study. Heroes can become role models. All children need them.

Outings:
- Visit the **Alamo** in San Antonio, Texas.
  - See a **movie** on the Alamo story.
  - **Maps,** diagrams.
  - **Stories** of the men.
  - Buy that **coonskin cap**.
- Visit **the San Jacinto Monument** in La Porte, Texas.
  - **Tell the story**. Read a book.
  - Sit out under the trees and imagine yourself in the story.
  - Yell: *Remember the Alamo! Remember Goliad!*

- Visit the museum (treasure hunt for some of the items)
- Role play with guns, hats, etc.
- Go to the top of the monument and see the land and layout. The older campers can identify the layout of the battlefield.
- See the movie documentary
- Don't forget the museum.

★ Visit Washington on the Brazos, Texas
- This is the site of the signing of the Declaration of Texas Independence. The original building is well-preserved, and the museum is interesting and educational.

★ Visit Palo Dura Canyon, Canyon, Texas.
- See the musical, "Texas," in the heart of the canyon. A rare experience.
- There is a great museum in Canyon Tx. That explores Texas history and its culture. You can engage children in this experience.

★ Stroll beaches.

★ Float a river.

Nana Camp

Gone to Texas

The history of Texas should include the stories of settlers who left their homes to follow Moses Austin to Texas. These early settlers boarded up their homes and businesses and left signs that said, "gone to Texas". Take your campers on an adventure and help them imagine what Texas looked like to those early settlers. Teach your campers how they lived, what they ate, how they traveled.

- Walk a forest, park and imagine what it was like.
- Walk a lone beach.
- Enjoy Galveston State Park (away from people).
- Float a river and have them look at the banks and imagine what the first settlers saw.
- Ride a horse!
- Visit a cave.
- Study the logistics: covered wagons, food, clothing.
- Try on pioneer clothes.
- Camp out. (If you are braver than I.).
- Tell stories of early settlers.
- Organize a scavenger hunt to spell the word "Texas." Find things in the yard that start with each letter.
- Learn Texas songs.
- Learn the pledge to the Texas flag
  Honor the Texas flag. I pledge allegiance to thee, Texas,
  One state under God, One and indivisible.

- ★ Wear cowboy clothes. There are plenty of museums and child-friendly places where they can actually put on the clothes.
- ★ Read the book, "Johnny Texas," a favorite of ours. (Hoff, Carol, *Johnny Texas*, Hendrick-Long Publishing Company, 1992)

All About Animals

This is a wide topic which sets the tone for a plethora of ideas to explore. (I'm sure your mind is already spinning with great ideas.) Animals are everywhere. The campers have outings everyday that involve finding, seeing, touching, and learning about animals. Then in the evening we ask, "what animals did you see today?" The lessons are limitless.

Activities:

- At the end of the outing, have children identify their favorite animal
- Draw that animal and have everyone guess what it is
- Tell a story about that animal
- Read books!!!
- Make animal puppets on a stick and perform a play.
- Watch animal movies, a great way to end the day.
- Catch lizards in the backyard.
- If you are fond of face painting, paint the campers' faces as their favorite animal!

Outings:

- **The zoo**—of course, the best source. Some zoos that opportunities to have a behind-the-scene visit with an animal and the zoo docent.
    - Don't just visit. Engage them.

- Ask campers beforehand what animals they want to see
- Have a scavenger hunt. Find items that you have chosen. Of course, this takes a little careful planning.
- Feed giraffes.
- Go "behind the scenes" so they can engage with the animal. Some zoos offer this opportunity for a charge.

★ **Veterinarian.** Visit your local veterinarian to learn how to care for your animals. (It really helps if your grandfather is a veterinarian as ours is.) Our campers get to go in with Poppy to handle animals, bathe them, and even observe surgery.

★ **SPCA.** Set up a visit to the local SPCA. (It also helps if your grandfather is on the board.) Tour the facility. The Houston SPCA has a fabulous wildlife rescue center. Our campers were able to go back and see the animals who were being treated. A couple of them decided they wanted to work there when they were old enough.

★ **Museum of Natural History.** Study insects, butterflies, and dinosaurs. Watch out for the docent who takes out the tarantulas and centipedes.
  - **IMAX.** There's always a wonderful movie starring animals at the Natural History Museum.

Bible story:
- ★ **Creation**

    God made man to rule over all the animals He had created. That meant naming them and taking care of them.

- ★ **Noah's ark**

    Tell the story of the flood. This could be done with flannelgraph, books, or a good movie version. Stories told with the help of a flannel board and felt pictures to place on the board are always engaging. The children might tell the stories and place the figures on the board.

    Talk about all that Noah had to do to care for all the animals.

The Lion of the Tribe of Judah

This was a venture into a wonderful theological truth about Jesus Christ, the Lion of the Tribe of Judah. The challenge was to convert this to children's theology and make it fun! It became a great, deep, creative exploration of "the lion"

Each day I set up the experience where they we saw or did something that involved a lion. At the end of the day I asked, "have you seen a lion today?" Campers list where they saw the lion, and as the week wore on, they began to look for lions. They would describe that lion. Tell me about it. What did it look like? What did it sound like? What was it doing? Where was it found? As they described the lion, we talked about what that lion tells us about Jesus, the Jewish rabbi/Son of God, the Messiah Who was born into the tribe of Judah and became "David's Greater Son." A lot to understand, yes! But they got it.

Activities:

- ★ Notebook. Prepare worksheets. Find pictures of lions to color and purchase stickers of lions. This takes some careful planning.

Nana Camp

Outings: (where to find these lions):

- ★ At the jumping **gym** there was a balloon lion above one of the blow ups. If you look around you will find them wherever you go.
- ★ The **zoo**.
- ★ **Movie.** *The Lion King* is a good place to start.
- ★ **Books**.
- ★ **The musical**, *Lion King,* came to Houston one year during Nana Camp. It was a great event and a grand evening full of lessons. (Again, this took careful planning with reservations and ticket purchases!)

We dressed up, went to a formal dinner before the theater and enjoyed a fabulous production. As a sidebar, at dinner we learned the art of manners and dinner conversation. At the theater we were in awe of the production.

This event became one of my favorite memories of Nana Camp. The children were enthralled. But my treasure came when we were preparing for our formal dinner before the production. We took the opportunity and learned how to dress for the theatre, how to conduct ourselves, how to have manners at the dinner table, and the art of dinner conversation. Five campers were directed to engage with the other dinner guests, looking at each person and asking a question or engaging in conversation in order to "mingle" with them. Another grandmother in our extended family asked if she could come for the evening with her two granddaughters, and of course, we said yes. When the last of our party arrived for dinner, Lily whispered to Jacob, "Now we have to mingle." They did!

Bible lessons:

Learn about Jewish people and the tribes of Israel
- Judah, the ruling tribe
- The lineage of Jesus

   Chart of the analogy between the lion and Jesus. This becomes a "type of Christ" to be recorded as worksheets in their notebooks. This requires help for little campers because it is a challenge for younger ones.

   It has become clear to me after working for 40 years in our children's ministry at church, that children of any age can learn the basic truths of the Word of God. When broken down into simple language and analogies, the great Truths of the Word can become clear in their souls. This is such a gift to give a child at an early age.

   This was the opportunity to teach more about the Lord Jesus Christ as He is revealed in Scripture.

The Lion	**Jesus**
Has a great mane	Is resplendent in glory
King of the jungle	King of Kings
Roars	Speaks with authority
Fierce when angered	Executes justice and judgment
Magnificent creature	Majestic creator
Head of his pride	Great God with absolute authority
Very powerful	Omnipotent
Protects and cares for his pride	Protects and cares for His children
Fights off predators	Fights our battles with the enemy

More About Texas (2013)

This year was 2013. After many years of Nana Camp, we returned to the theme of Texas history. We had two new campers (Georgia and Joseph) who had never heard the story according to Nana. Two more campers (Lily and Jacob) had not heard the story in years, and the two older campers (Josh and Jackson) knew the story very well.

One can go back to the native Indians and early explorers. The grandmother who is a lover of Texas history will love this curriculum, and it is great fun for the campers.

When Nana Camp studies Texas history we "own" it! Campers understand their state and its legacy, all presented with the principle that "Jesus Christ controls history." Little ones learn about the flag with one star. Older ones learn the facts and stories of the participants. When my oldest grandson went to junior high school, he was given the assignment to write a paper on the battle of San Jacinto. When he laughed and was asked what was so funny, he answered, "I could do this from memory. I've been to Nana Camp!"

Here I reiterate that notebooks are important. After we arrived at Uncle David's and Aunt Melissa's house in Boerne, Texas, we got our suitcases arranged and had our first "camp meeting." We herded all campers into the playroom where we had set out their notebooks, backpacks, and other supplies. This would be our gathering room, set up much like a campfire. We did a quick orientation of "all about Texas" and rushed off to explore the first cave which was nearby.

Outings:

- ★ We went to the ***Cave without a Name*** near Boerne, Texas. It was quite an adventure. Joseph (five years old) was excited about his second year at Nana Camp until he saw the dark hole with steep steps going down to the huge hole in the ground. This is where you jump on the opportunity to discuss principles and promises. Nana explained, "I will be there and not leave you. Jesus is with you all the time and He will take care of you. Trust Him when you are afraid. We are here and you ARE going." Well, Nana carried him down the steep (really steep!) stairs screaming, and once we hit the bottom step and the lights came on, he let go of her hand and said, "*Wow! This is great. I love this!!!!*" Fear conquered; Nana exhausted. Worth the effort! Lesson learned!

    In this cave we entered a massive cavern. The guide asked if anyone sang. Of course, Joshua (grandchild #3) has a beautiful voice and had performed solo in a church service back in Lubbock. We became quiet and he sang *Blessed Assurance, Jesus is mine*. It was a stunning performance in a large cavern with perfect acoustics. I'm pretty sure the Lord designed that moment for me. Remember, that is one of my "songs." I will forever remember that moment tucked into Nana Camp.

★ The second cave was ***Natural Bridge Caverns***—big and spacious—and we went with a tour guide. Other activities there included zip lines for the older campers and a playground for the younger ones. On the way back to Boerne we ate at a fun place and discussed our adventures. This is where I would ask, "what was your favorite thing today?" Oh, the great conversations that follow.

★ The **Alamo**, always a must-see, is an icon of Texas history with much to learn about those famous heroes.

★ View the **IMAX movie**, *Price of Freedom*, which is appropriate for even the young campers. It is visual, but has never bothered my campers even as young as four years old. This is a great place to launch the discussion of "freedom through military victory."

★ **SeaWorld** is another great adventure. Though not really part of Texas curriculum, we just had to go because it was in San Antonio.

All About the Wind

Now, this was really creative! We took Nana Camp to Lubbock in 2014 and learned about early Texas settlers and the plains Indians. Incorporated in this adventure was the theme, THE WIND. After all, there is lots of wind on the South Plains.

Activities:

- Make **pinwheels**.
- Put **large pinwheels** in the yard and hope the wind blows so you can watch them spin.

Outings:

- The **Lubbock Farm and Ranch Heritage Museum** is located just outside the campus of Texas Tech. This museum has a wonderful collection of authentic dwellings from the cave houses built into the dirt hillside to large ranch houses. There is even a train to explore.
- At the R.E. Janes **Gravel Plant** in Slaton, Texas, (it helps if your uncle is the owner!) we learned about rocks and climbed huge gravel mountains. It was a great day of exploration.
- The **Wind Mill Museum** in Lubbock is a wonderful attraction.

- ★ The trip to **Palo Duro Canyon** provided a great and memorable evening. The musical, *"Texas"* is performed on the stage in the canyon.
- ★ A Jeep tour into the canyon was both fun and educational. Years ago, we toured an Indian teepee in the canyon.
- ★ The **History Museum in Canyon, TX** is a great museum that we had visited in the past. We learned about Indians and their way of life as well as early Texas settlers from a reconstructed Western town which was new to the museum.

Bible story: Jesus calming the storm.

"Who is this (what manner of man is this) that even the winds and the seas obey Him." Mark 4:41

Jesus was asleep in the boat. He was the picture of confidence. The question: will you trust this One Who controls the winds and the seas as well as everything in your life? Live like you know the One in the boat with you. This is a picture of the faith-rest life. (Thieme, R. B. Jr, "The Faith-Rest Life, R.B. Thieme Jr. Bible Ministries, 1961.) The Bible lesson on the Holy Spirit included John 3:8. Campers learned that *"the wind blows where it wills."* A child can understand that you can feel the wind and see its powerful force and effects. We can't see the Holy Spirit, but we can see how He works and trust His power.

The wind and the Holy Spirit are powerful. We can suffer under this power or we can prosper. The choice is ours and our obedience to Him and the Word of God. This provides opportunity for developing a study of the Person and work of the Holy Spirit.

The Arts (2017)

Location: back in Houston at Nana's house. This offered the opportunity to explore all sorts of fine arts. First we had to define "the arts" for our camp. We settled on: *anything that creates beauty or inspiration.*

Verse: "*God created the heavens and the earth.*" Genesis 1:1. He is the greatest artist.

Activities:
- ★ We painted, drew, worked in our art books at home. It was a very creative experience. We collected these works in our portfolios which we made at the beginning of camp.
- ★ There were numerous crafts where they made their own art. At the end of camp we had an art show for parents. We discovered that there are artists among us! And there are others who are NOT.

Outings:
- ★ **The George Theater** where the A.D. Players performed "The Lion, the Witch, and the Wardrobe" was very engaging. We watched the movie the night before and talked about the book.
- ★ We visited **a local Houston artist** who is the artist in residence at Houston Baptist University. Michael

Collins was very gracious to invite us into his studio and his home. It was a fabulous experience with a renowned artist.

★ **An art lesson** for each camper was a highlight. We visited the studio of Houston artist, Hanh Tran. There the four campers had an art lesson and produced beautiful works of art, directed by the artist, to take home.

Girl time in Texas (2018)

The location for this year was San Antonio, a great place to explore Texas history. We set up camp at the home of my niece, Jill, whose two little girls had joined our Nana Camp. My last two campers, Georgia and Genny, were 9 and 5 in 2018. It proved to be a bit difficult to conduct our developed Nana Camp protocol with just two little girls. It was a perfect time for two second cousins to join us. Lila and Cora were the perfect ages (7 and 4) to enter our camp experience. With four little girls it was great to tweak the study of Texas history to highlight what it must have been like for little girls to travel to Texas and grow up in the new country.

Pass it on. My oldest granddaughter, Lily was 13 this year and became our first official counsellor-in-training. She helped, encouraged, fielded questions, fixed "broken" knees, organized games, and even led in presenting a worksheet to go in their notebooks. It was motivating for little girls who love her, great training for her, a look into the path on which she would surely travel as a teacher/counsellor. The legacy is being passed down.

Activities:

- ★ Lots of **worksheets** from color books that teach about longhorn cattle, mustangs, Indians, explorers, the Texas motto (Friendship), the meaning of Texas (friends, allies), the Texas flag which they color and

then draw and color from memory, the seal of the state, state bird, flower, the six flags over Texas, etc. Let your imagination and your resources explode.
- ★ Learn the **pledge to the Texas flag**.
Honor the Texas flag. I pledge allegiance to thee, Texas, One state under God, one and indivisible.
- ★ Learn the **Texas song**.
Texas, our Texas, all hail the mighty State!
Texas, our Texas, so wonderful so great!
Boldest and grandest, withstanding every test
O empire wide and glorious, you stand supremely blessed.
God bless you Texas! And keep you brave and strong,
That you may grow in power and worth throughout the ages long.
God bless you Texas and keep you brave and strong
That you may grow in power and worth, throughout the ages long.

Remember, all of these make wonderful worksheets for their notebooks.
- ★ **Press flowers**. Little girls in early Texas did not have the recreational resources that our grandchildren have. So they were creative! Our girls went on a walk and picked flowers of their choosing. Then we pressed them carefully and let them sit for a day. The girls were thrilled with their creations. Nana had the frames ready and we placed the pressed

flowers in them to take to their homes. I see them displayed in their rooms and in my home!
- **Make a band of flowers** for their hair, or purchase them.
- **Make a homemade doll**. Little girls in early Texas had dolls made from anything they could find. We saw those at the Alamo gift shop made from corncobs, treasures for those little girls.
- **Prepare food** that would have worked on the trail rides.
- **Visit the Rainforest Café**—just for fun! This has nothing to do with Texas history, but it's near the Alamo.
- **Tie dye** shirts—again, just for fun.
- **Make a cake** decorated like the Texas flag.

For those grandmothers who don't live in Texas, research is easily available on the history of their states and the special places to visit. Every one of our 50 states has a wonderful history to explore and embrace. Better yet, come to Texas!

Outings:
- **The Alamo** is a great study of the fight for Texas independence. There are wonderful books, resources, games, and training aids of all kinds. A look at these Texas heroes and their stories is our state's legacy.

It is good to prepare the campers beforehand and prepare them for what to look for in the mission.
- ★ The **gift store** is a wealth of treasures. Our rule is "only one item may be purchased, so choose wisely."
- ★ Again, before visiting the Alamo, watch **the movie** at the IMAX across the street in the River Center, "*Price of Freedom.*" It is a must. Now, I recommended this to the grandfather who has Camp Pops with his grandchildren. (Remember, while the mothers shopped with Grandmother?) I assured him that it was not bloody. Well, his granddaughter disagreed. Lesson learned: do your own investigation. I always leave this movie with tears of appreciation for those men who sacrificed their lives, teaching my campers that "freedom is not free." Yes, my girls all shed tears of appreciation for these men and their state.
★ **Explore a cave.** Ask who were the first people in Texas to find these caves. Some have markings on the walls. We love:
  - ★ Natural Bridge Caverns. There is a lot to do there including zip lines, a maze, and a place to have lunch.
  - ★ Cave without a Name in Boerne, Texas.
  - ★ Longhorn Cavern.

Sea Creatures (2019)

Location: beach house at the coast on Mustang Island (2019) or Nana's house in Houston where we could access Galveston. We have done both in different years.

Activities:
- **Create Sand art** with sand from the beach or colored sand which has been purchased. It can be put in containers, glued on wood, paper or any other surface.
- **Collect shells.**
- **Make sandcastles.**
- **Write in the sand and take pictures.**
- **Fish, surf.**
- **The activities are endless.**

Outings:
- **Observe the turtle release.** This must coordinate with the schedule of the turtle rescue organization, but is well worth the effort.
- The **Texas Aquarium**, Corpus Christi.
- **Reg Dragon Pirate Ship** Excursion in Port Aransas.
- **Boat trip** over to St. Joe's Island from Mustang Island.
- **Harbor Tours** on Mustang Island.

- **Sea World** (if you are in San Antonio, Texas).
- **Rainforest Café** in Galveston.
- Historic **Harbor Tours** and Dolphin Watch in Galveston, Texas.

Each "Nana Camp" has become an adventure in itself. Each experience is different. I believe that the best is yet to come! I am reminded with the statement, "and it came to pass" of all that is involved in those words. With the process, the details, the challenges, the people involved, the subject matter, the lessons, I am confident that God's plan never wavers off course. "And it came to pass." There is much included as He covers the space with His perfect provision. Romans 8:28 says that "all things work together for good." He is doing that even now, and I can trust His Sovereignty at such a time as this. "And it came to pass." He is certainly in the midst of the process. In my life, Nana Camp is part of that process with my grandchildren.

Bible story: Jonah and the Whale

The Moon, Sun, and Stars (2020)

With this writing, I have faced the limitations of the COIVID 19 virus as the state has put many restrictions on gatherings. The theme for Nana Camp 2020 was Space, the moon, sun, and stars. Now, I did not know much about space, but I dug into research and learned. Actually, four little girls (ages 6 to 11) taught me much about the subject. With this interesting turn of events, we had a wonderful week with many doors that opened to us.

I guess my great lesson was to be flexible! That means being flexible in the non-essentials and non-flexible in the essentials. The non-essentials were where we went, what we could actually do, and where we would eat. For instance, this year included "no pools," "no close eating quarters," "no shopping," and no NASA. So, Nana collected all sorts of crafts, projects, and worksheets we could do at home. Of course, that meant no field trips and lots of home cooked meals.

The essentials with which we would NOT be flexible included the lessons we learned from God's Word, the doctrinal conclusions from movies we watched, and any project that would deviate from what we know to be Truth from the Bible.

So, with our focus in mind, we put on our masks, sanitized our hands, and carried on.

Nana Camp

The focus was three components: space, man in space, and the essence of God over space. We studied our solar system with all kinds of props and pictures, planets, constellations, and movies of men going into space.

Location: Nana's house in Houston, Texas. Of course, we thought NASA and the Space Center would surely be part of our adventures.

Activities:

- Color **pillow cases** and visors.
- **Cleaning**. Because of COVID protocols, we cleaned door handles, counters, and anything they would touch. I learned that they can be good cleaners!
- **Camp t-shirts**. Georgia designed t-shirts that were given to all campers, Nana, Aunt Jill, and Memow. Her t-shirt read *"Girls need space."* Nana expanded this to include a worksheet where they learned that "space" means three things:
  - The vast expanse that provides air for us to breathe, sunshine for light and warmth, beauty to behold.
  - Individual space that we all need at some time. This can be just when you need to be alone. You need to create that space when you feel in danger and need to put space between yourself and the object, or space from someone

who is "bugging you." Of course, this led to wonderful discussion and Biblical application of what this means.
  - ★ Quiet space which is your alone, private, quiet time with your God. This includes Bible study, praise with music, prayer, and anything that includes that special time with you and the Lord.
- ★ **Plaster of Paris hands.** With plaster of Paris we made forms of each girls' hand. Then with play dough they fashioned small planets from our solar system and placed them in the hand, representing God's Hand holding it all together.
- ★ **Star gazing.** Again, the Lord surprised us! We had clear nights which is not always the case in Houston. During this week we learned that Saturn and Jupiter would be seen in the southeastern sky. Sure enough, at bedtime there they were. Absolutely amazing.
- ★ **Rock painting** (to look like planets). You should see our solar system.
- ★ **Cookie painting.** Again, planets
- ★ **Puzzle** of our solar system
- ★ **Constellations** shown on a projector and drawn on worksheets
- ★ **Crocs.** This took a little prior planning. Nana ordered each girl a pair of crocs with the deco-

rations, called "jibitz," to be attached. I put them out on the table and the girls took turns choosing their jibitz. It was a great success and their shoes made a great fashion statement.

★ **Dress up**. From my dress up chest upstairs and with a little help from Nana's closet, the girls dressed for a "proper tea." It was hilarious and extremely creative on their parts. The great fun was in creating their individual portraits which would revealed in their camp books once Nana gets them made.

★ Blow-up **swimming pool**. Since we could not go to a pool, we played games in a small (really, pretty large) pool.
  ★ Duck races with a balloon to propel them. Blow up a balloon and use that air to propel the duck.
  ★ Water balloons
  ★ Be creative!

★ **Make-a-plate**. This year we all contributed to one plate with rockets, the sun, flowers, etc on the plate. Each girl will receive the same plate.

★ **Letter-writing**. Letters were written to a couple of people who have been involved in Nana Camp but who could not come this year. Each girl also received a letter from a "alumni camper." I had four of my older grandchildren write a special letter to the four youngest. When they opened those

letters, they were "over the moon." Such a special word from an older cousin, and a precious way to encourage that "cousin bond."
* **American girl dolls**. Each girl brought her doll. (You could not do this if boy cousins were involved!!) They dressed them, with one doll being the astronaut who would go to the moon. Yes, I had the flight suit!! We had the photographer, the computer person, and lots of observers.

Outings:

Trusting the Lord is the largest component of Nana Camp and the model of faith-rest. The girls knew that NASA was not open and our trip to Galveston for the night was definitely out. But, enter God's surprise! By the time the last day arrived, it was announced that NASA would open for members only with proper protocols in place. Can you imagine the collective cries of joy? We quickly got reservations and were the third group to enter the pristine, newly redesigned, COVID-safe Space Center. It was great to actually see what we had studied. And the other surprise which delighted the girls is that a major news channel was there for the opening and interviewed us as first visitors. So, Nana Camp made the 4:00 news. It was a great experience and the girls were so excited—as was Nana. Our news reporter was very interested in Nana Camp.

- **Ceramic painting.** We did get to go to the Mad Potter with masks and social distancing.
- **Eating out** one time was a treat.

Bible verse:
- Psalm 19:1 "The heavens declare the glory of God; and the skies proclaim the work of His hands."
- Genesis 1:1 "In the beginning, God created…."
- We studied the character of God as it relates to creation and holding the universe together. Sovereignty, omnipotence, omniscience
- A great resource which we found on UTUBE was Louis Giglio's video, "*Indescribable.*"

It is my desire to continue this adventure of Nana Camp as long as the Lord allows.

Chapter 6

Find a sidekick, a Tonto, a "Memow"

★ ★ ★

My mother had a precious sister who "did life" with her and a best friend who lived on our street. Her sister, Mary, was very close to my mother, and therefore, to us. My aunt became my confident, my encourager, the wise woman who modeled for me a life lived in obedience to the Word. She was a pastor's wife for ten years and taught Bible class. I wanted to "be" her. She poured her love and wisdom into my life. She opened my eyes to see Jesus. I learned from another of my mentors that God did not want me to be "Mary." He already had one. He wanted to use Marsha.

The women in my life have had best friends who walked with them, encouraged them, came along side to be used of the Lord in good times and bad.

My best friend, Jane Marmion, wanted to have more grandchildren than just the one, Maric. As God would have it, she opened her life and her heart to my eight. She is their "Memow," a name of affection given to her by her grandson. (not to be confused with meow, the sound her pet cat made.)

One of the blessings of our relationship is that we model for them a faithful friendship. Many women have confided in me that they wish they had a "Jane." Grounded in the Word of God, they see in our friendship ties that create a life-long friendship that truly lasts until eternity. The secret is certainly the Word of God working in each of our souls.

Proverbs 17:7 says, a *"friend loveth at all times."*

There is a wealth of doctrine to be unpacked in that one word, friend. Our testimony is that as long as we have God's Word in our souls, it works!

Jane comes alongside me and helps with Nana Camp. She is a valuable asset, and I have watched through the years different grandchildren connect to her in a special way that I could not see. She ministers to them and their individual needs.

When Hunter was just four and Maric was 5, Jane and I began "Camp memow/Nana" with two little grandsons. When others saw our efforts, we were joined by a great Aunt and her great nephew. Later, that camp extended to little girls, friends whom we had embraced. Their parents were overjoyed with the time we spent and wisdom we poured into four little girls for many years.

Later when Camp became all-consuming, we carried on with my grandchildren, thus redesigned into Nana

Camp. As each one was born and became four years old, they cycled through this great adventure.

Sidekicks can be prayer partners. As we have seen its great benefit, it continues to be a rich blessing to have a friend who is committed to the power of prevailing prayer. She (or he) becomes one who sends up a barrage of prayer support that the Lord answers according to His will. Eternity will tell the many ways prayer has interceded in the journey of Nana Camp.

Every year we take this show "*On the road again.*"

Travel creates a special kind of bond in the process. Have you noticed the community that surrounds air travel or cruise travel? You watch each other, watch out for each other, and often find great comradery in conversation. If a challenge occurs there is a bonding that your fellow traveler experiences with those in community.

When Nana Camp goes on the road there is a community created. Cooperation must be foremost to make the journey better. Helping each other is critical. Watching out for the other traveler is part of the journey. I love to see grandchildren, young and old, enter the journey of travel. Holding hands, singing songs, watching younger ones across the street are just examples of what can occur in group travel. It enriches life's journey.

In the car we establish a protocol. Once we are securely in our seats with our backpacks near, we begin the adventure with songs that I have recorded on the radio such as *"on the road again"* and *"it's a grand ole flag."* Drawing picture in our notepads is a visual way of documenting their journey. Helping each other creates strong community.

When your two hands are on the wheel, your sidekick can help the campers with their needs.

Jane has been my friend for over fifty years. We were young college beauties (ha!) when we met. We have aged with great memories along the way. You are as young as you think. I believe I first read those words in a book by Douglas McArthur, and I did not appreciate them until I reached my 70s. I do not think or feel "old". I have to be reminded of what I should and should not do!

That perspective serves me well when it comes to being Nana. While I do not identify with much of the perspective of this generation, I aspire to listen and relate while waiting for the opportunity to offer my opinions. My generation of "baby boomers" is encouraged to "remain active." I do that. The motivation to engage with my grandchildren keeps me moving, active, and participating. It's great exercise.

> **Prayer:** Oh, Lord, may I continue with this energy and strength! Claiming, "I can do all things though Christ Who strengthens me." Phil. 4 (well, almost anything!)

Nana Camp

"Wisdom is with the aged men, with long life is understanding." JOB 12:12

"May he (Obed) also be to you a restorer of life and a sustainer of your old age; for your daughter-in-law who loves you and is better to you than seven sons, has given birth to him." RUTH 4:15

"For the righteous man will flourish like the palm tree. He will grow like a cedar in Lebanon. Planted in the house of the Lord, they will flourish in the courts of our God. They will still yield fruit in old age." PSALM 92:12–15

"O, God, Thou hast taught me from my youth; and I still declare Thy wondrous deeds. And even when I am old and gray, O God, do not forsake me, until I declare Thy strength to this generation." PSALM 71: 17–18

One of my prayers in the past was that I would never be so old that I did not remember what it was like to be young. Now, there's a mouthful. We probably don't do that as well when we are parenting. We are concentrating on raising our children with protocols, values and standards, regardless of what the culture shouts at them. While the same is true today, I practice the exercise of remembering what I felt like at the age of my grandchildren when they are facing dilemmas. When they are insecure and lacking self-confidence before entering their teens, I identify. I remember those feelings and how the Lord molded me through them. It really helps with my prayer life and in talking to them.

I don't think my grandmother ever "got old." At 86, she was as fun and engaged with my grandchildren as she was with me when she dressed up like Minnie Pearl, complete with the price tag on her hat, coming to visit my friends who had come for a slumber party. Remember, my grandchildren are her GREAT grandchildren. They loved her, laughed with her, and found her just plain fun. They all remember her in the back part of a van the year we took her to Florida with us. "*Country Road, Take me Home*" was the song we bellowed when it came on the radio, and they all sang with her—with great gusto. Of course, my friends as well as my children's friends remember. They loved her and her spirit. I think she is a mentor to me in the "art of having fun."

One of my life quotes is from Chuck Swindoll. "Live in joyful excess, and smile, inviting others to join the party." I hope the Lord has told Grandmother that I am doing just that.

Chapter 7
The Extended Blessings of Nana Camp

★ ★ ★

The gift to parents: time alone.

One of my daughters-in-law, Emily Griffith, had seen me conduct Nana Camp, but when it came time for her four-year-old to attend, she just couldn't send Georgia with me to Boerne, Texas. She did not want her to leave her mom and dad, which is understandable for a first-child. So, of course, we prayed and asked the Lord how to handle this. I invited Emily, the mom, to come with us. She could stay at home with the other moms, Caroline and Melissa, or she could go everywhere we went. She did both. We conducted Nana Camp, 2013 in the midst of all the moms and dads at my son and daughter-in-law, David and Melissa's home in Boerne.

Now when summer is approaching, Emily, the reluctant mom, is the first to ask, "When is Nana Camp?" She and my son plan their little get-always during this time. Now we seldom hear from them except to say "hello."

During camp time when I am responsible for their children, parents now have time alone again—to reflect on their marriages without the busy days of children. They connect while their children are having a special dedicated time. I am supporting and nourishing their marriage with my gift to them—time.

One year my daughter, Caroline and her husband, Jason, gave us their home in Lubbock to conduct Nana Camp while she and her husband went to Cabo San Lucas. Now, that's taking advantage of time alone and time away.

For me, one of the extended blessings of Nana Camp has been watching my older grandchildren recall little things (and big things!) they remember from their time at Nana Camp. All of my eight grandchildren have a tendency to embrace and do well with history. I am inclined to think they are products of those years we studied history of all sorts.

The first time Hunter was asked to write a paper on Texas history his teacher assigned him the Battle of San Jacinto. He just laughed and declared, "I don't even need to research this! I've been there. I've been to Nana Camp."

In 2019 all of my family were at the coast for the 4th of July. With a group on the balcony of a beach home watching the fireworks in the distance, Hunter, who was then 20, started singing *"America the Beautiful."* With four of his cousins and his sister surrounding a few adults the entire group joined him. Before I knew it, they were singing fun songs from Nana Camp and laughing at the words that they had so proudly learned in the car as little ones. Now as adults they were proclaiming loudly with their small cousins: *"all God's children got a place in the choir...."* I will forever cherish that memory of the blending of those voices from past days. Such moments create precious memories for me.

Another blessing of Nana Camp is the opportunity to share with parents what they have done and learned. Every year the families get the Shutterfly memory book filled with pictures of their days, quotes, pictures from the stories they learned, actual pictures they drew, and sometimes pictures of their worksheets. Parents love to enjoy and encourage conversation from these books. And they are great records of past Nana Camps.

I have observed, as a result of time spent at Nana Camp, deeper connections these cousins have formed. Their leadership skills are nurtured. Lily has become a wonderful mentor/counsellor to the younger girls. I can see the development of her spiritual gifts, and will be excited to see how the Lord uses her. With our wide span in ages, there are cousins who never attended Nana Camp together, but they still have the experience in common and can build on that.

There is a special gift you can give to your grandchildren: create a special weekend (or moment) for **their** mothers. I love to plan "girl-time" just for moms. We have been to resorts, spas, the beach, my home where no children are allowed! Conferences such as" Inspire Women" or "Women of Faith" are great venues. Concerts, events, shopping are also fun times together. Sometimes just being together and going nowhere is the best. Plan it and then stand back and see what happens with the mommies. First of all, the dads will call with a thousand questions until they figure out that they can solve these logistical problems on their own.

When women gather amazing things happen. When women of God gather, there are eternal results. The encouragement, understanding and support are valuable blessing to these ladies. Our family provides times for the "girls" to gather. Oh, the wisdom that comes when women are transparent. I have seen so many issues identified and addressed among women. Remember the women in antiquity who gathered at the well? Well, it is my commitment to provide gatherings that don't involve drawing water!

I am blessed by the writing of this book. The exercise of recording my thoughts has given me great appreciation for the journey on which I have traveled. I love those who have been part of my life, and am very grateful for their support and encouragement. The Lord has blessed me with amazing people, including you, the reader. It's a blessing to be able to "do" life together. I appreciate you, the reader, and continue to cherish the many stories you have shared with me about your grandchildren. I am sorry to see this book end because I have included a few of your stories, but I intend to continue collecting your adventures.

> ***Prayer:*** give my children wisdom, energy, direction to raise their children under God's authority

> ***Prayer:*** Bless the reader of this book. May each one receive encouragement from You, just as I have.

Chapter 8
Source of strength: Jesus

★ ★ ★

It's really not about me.
It's really all about Him.
My children and grandchildren know that.
Nurture their souls.

Of course, this is the primary responsibility of their parent. I would never get in the way of that relationship, nor would they allow me. Because I know the boundaries of a grandmother, I am blessed to have the invitation of my children to speak into the lives of theirs. The role of a grandparent is not the role of the parent. One of the most powerful things I can offer them is my prayer support.

> ***Prayer:*** give my children wisdom, energy, direction to raise their children under God's authority

One of the most powerful ways to encourage and reinforce their walks is the times they fail, and they will. Look back on their parents, but don't tell their stories!

Failure is part of life, and certainly a subject that must be addressed when walking the Christian life. God provides for our failures. After all, He took care of the sin issue on the cross. That becomes the basis for all recovery, forgiveness, and moving on.

Our "perfect" grandchildren will soon prove to be not so perfect! I remember the story of George H. W. Bush encouraging one of his grandsons at a time of personal and public failure. The letter of encouragement that President Bush wrote to that grandson was one of the remembrances offered at the President's funeral.

The first information that comes to grandparents of their grandchildren's failures usually comes from their parents. My grandchildren have not often confessed to me their failures, especially not the big ones. My children will often come with prayer requests and requests for wise counsel. Prayer is my first "attack." I often intercede and ask that the Lord will open their eyes, remind them of His grace recovery, and deal with their consequences in that grace. Remember when Moses interceded for the children of Israel in the wilderness and the Lords spared them? Undergirding those parents on the battle line is critical.

> ***Prayer:*** Lord, may I always be ready to give wise counsel because of the doctrine in my soul. Make it Your counsel, not mine.

Those not-so-perfect grandchildren will often face us with their mistakes and failures. There is the moment of truth when you assure them of God's forgiveness and yours. I watched my mother and father when my children were horrified that their grandparents would find out about their blunders. They had to be accountable to the people who loved them so much and wanted them to be the best they could be. I appreciated the gravity of their having to "admit" and face these grandparents they so admired. In our case, my parents understood God's grace recovery. The grace and forgiveness mirrored that of their Heavenly Father. The admonition to turn to Him and move forward was invaluable. Always run to Him, not away.

> ***Prayer:*** Lord, let my life be a reflection of your limitless grace. You have forgiven me and restored me time and again. May they receive grace and forgiveness from me and know how to walk with You.

> ***Prayer:*** When failure happens let them know as I do to always run to You, never away in shame.

Even when they're so bad and you're so mad there is a great moment of truth and life lessons. The year that we studied Jonah and the whale I went to great extremes to explain what happened to Jonah in that belly. They were quite taken with the fact that the big fish swallowed the disobedient prophet and then spit him up. I taught Jonah's failure and recovery. We discussed, did worksheets, and imagined how sorry Jonah was. I emphasized that Jonah confessed his sins and sought God's forgiveness which was freely given. I felt that they were more impressed with the story than with the great lesson of forgiveness which is offered to us on a regular basis in the spiritual life.

I even blindfolded them in the yard and poured all manner of food stuffs on them to show them that it was not a fun experience to be in a fish's belly. That became a great adventure that they still talk about!

Then came the last day of Nana camp when we went to a movie. Well, as we were leaving the theater their sin natures all erupted at the same time. They became incorrigible and would not respond to Nana's harsh words of correction. When we dissolved into force, we marched to the car in silence where they were verbally reprimanded. Disobedience is not cool. When we got home, I told them to go to their rooms, think about their disobedience, and not come down until they had confessed their personal sins to God the Father and then were ready to apologize to me and to Memow.

Well, that year my daughter was staying with us in the house and she heard everything. She instructed her boys to write apologies to Nana when they were ready. The girls heard this instruction and took notice. I received the most incredible letters and pictures of apology. One simply said, "Nana, I'm sorry I acted like a fool." We still laugh about that one!

As they came downstairs one by one with letters in hand, I looked at their eyes and said, "I forgive you as your Heavenly Father has forgiven you. Now let's have a great evening."

The next day I asked Lily what was her favorite thing about Nana Camp. She named a few things and then said, "I did not like yesterday." I explained that it was hard, but it was a great lesson of what happens when we fail and sin. 1 John 1:9 tells us that *"if we confess our sins He is faithful and just to forgive us our sins and to cleanse us from all unrighteousness"*. Sins forgiven; fellowship restored. The life lesson taught them so much more than what I was trying to present with the story of Jonah. I marvel at how the Lord accomplishes the supernatural in His right time! Again, lessons learned.

You must know your subject. Be prepared, know the Word of God. His plan is the only way.

> ***Prayer:*** May I hear the Word you have for me—inaudibly but clearly—that I might obey with confidence.

God is not impressed if you make up stuff as you go along. He is impressed when we surrender and apply His Word through His power.

Chapter 9

One More Thing (in a nutshell)

★ ★ ★

"Becoming a grandmother is wonderful. One moment you're just a mother. The next you are all-wise and prehistoric." (Brown, Pam, "Grandmothers are a Gift from God, Zondervan Publishing House, 1973, p. 88) This title is truly the label of a grand adventure. Any one of could get carried away in our role. There are a few more things we should remember.

Never ever assume the role of the parent. We are not their parents!

We support the parent.

We offer wise counsel to the parent.

We ask the grandchild's parents' permission when in doubt. We follow their parents' rules.

We define boundaries of a grandparent. This defines who I am and who I am not.

Wonderful books have been written about having appropriate boundaries in life. We are wise when we understand what that means.

> ***Prayer:*** Let me define appropriate boundaries with my grandchildren so that I can be an influence in their lives without interfering with the role of their parents.

There are for many different reasons, those great exceptions, those blessed and noble grandparents who raise their grandchildren. We have heard those stories. The reasons vary as to why parents abdicate their privilege. Bravo to those grandparents who step in. The task is great; the burden is greater. The age factor certainly becomes an issue. But I believe the Lord gives special strength and encouragement to those grandparents. I'm sure their love would not allow any other option.

If you are not a grandparent, you can still celebrate. You had one. I would encourage you, dear reader, to take a moment and remember your grandmothers. If you did not know them you can only speculate from their history. If you were blessed to know them, consider the impact they had on your life. Who were they? How do they make you feel today when you think of them? What was the legacy they left? Thank the Lord for giving you these women, for He makes no mistakes.

I have celebrated both of my grandmothers in various ways. I have pictures of these two women in my home, pictures that my grandchildren can see as I relate their stories. I have objects of china, silver services, furniture, and treasures that were theirs. I have jewelry that I have passed down with pictures to identify the women who graced these pieces. We remember!

In the senerio that you will never be a grandmother, there is an easy solution if you care to explore it. Find a child who needs one! Ask the Lord for the assignment, for it must come from Him. Some children who don't have grandparents or don't have ones that want to leave an imprint on their lives might need you. There is always a child who needs someone. I think of the couples who adopt children, of the CASA volunteer who walks into the life of a child, of the special friends who take an interest. That someone could be you.

I had two wonderful grandmothers, but my Neenie took me as hers. She was my grandmother's sister, and I was her special person from birth. She had no children of her own, but she had me. Juanita Nesbit left an indelible imprint on my soul.

As I have pondered the phenomena of a grandmother, I have taken the liberty to explore a purely hypothetical question supported by facts that we do know from the Bible. This venture is pure speculation. What we do know is that in His humanity, Jesus Christ had two grandmothers. He was born to a man and a woman, one who gave Him His natural grandmother, and one who gave Him an adopted grandmother. We know that because He was true humanity, He grew up in a home with normal interactions with family, and He would have likely known these women if they were alive. I wonder how He how He would have related to these aging women. Can you imagine His love and respect for them? As Jesus "*grew in wisdom and stature and in favor with God and man,*" (Luke 2:52), He would have listened and learned from them. Grandmothers would have taught the boy about his ancestry, and what a lineage He did have! The stories gleamed from the names listed in the line of the tribe of Judah were amazing. I can imagine young Jesus sitting at their feet, fascinated by the people who went before Him in His humanity. He would have embodied the loving relationship between a grandmother and her grandson, unique as He was. As a grandmother, I celebrate that moment, and will not know until eternity when I see Him if He actually knew these women. Fun to consider!

We do know that the families of Abraham, Isaac, and Jacob lived and traveled in close proximity to each other. I would love to hear the stories of the grandchildren of Sarah, Rebekah, and Rachel as they lived their daily lives. Perhaps those women as grandmothers would say, "you did WHAT?"

We also know, if only briefly, the grandmother of Timothy in the New Testament. The living conditions in his home have been discussed in a previous chapter. With Lois and Eunice caring for him in that first century home, what an amazing life he must have had with his grandmother. She and his mother trained him well.

Many grandmothers are engaged in powerful careers that demand their time and attention. The exercise of Nana Camp is perfect for them. One of my friends has beloved great nephews who live far away from her. Nana Camp is perfect for her. Many grandmothers are caregivers for their parents. Nana Camp is perfect for them. To devote even a few days a year to an intentional time with your grandchildren is a gift they will never forget. Pick a subject, create your own, and go for it!

While sharing these thoughts with a friend, she asked what I would say to a grandparent who lives far away from grandchildren and is not able to see them. Perhaps it is financially impossible to travel. Perhaps health limitations keep one from visits. Perhaps busy schedules don't allow for visits. Or just maybe your children or in-laws don't want you to be part of your grandchildren's lives. There are many reasons that keep grandparents from regular visits.

To this scenario I would answer that if a grandmother's heart desires to be in her grandchildren's lives, there is always hope that this will happen. The first line of attack I would suggest is prayer. We have heard many times a person say, "I know my grandmother prayed for me." God answers the desires of our hearts. He often requires obedience to Him first, especially if He is showing us how to change our approach, actions or behavior.

In today's frantic world, there is the option of technology in the form of skype, texts, phone calls, email messages, or (imagine!) hand-written letters. The mail service gives us the opportunity to include pictures, books, and all kinds of gifts that remind the child that you are available, think of them and love them.

My step-daughter, Kary, recently found in a box many letters sent to her throughout her life from her grandmother, Lorine Eckermann. My mother-in-law has been with the Lord for many years. I knew her as a very kind and gracious lady. I did not know that she wrote letters to her grandchildren. While these children lived in Houston, she lived in a nearby county in the old family home on the hill. Those letters written in her beautiful hand were treasures to those grandchildren as they came in the mail addressed to them individually. One of her comments to the granddaughter who was growing up in the city read, "take care and watch out for the crazy people. Only look for the good ones." Now, that is a gift, and contains advice I could write to my grandchildren today. This gift of words has been recycled again to Kary, so many years later as she opened that box of letters. My grandmother, Odia, did the same. It made me want to go to my attic and find some of those cards and letters from her.

Where there is difficulty in the relationship it is always a good idea to go through the parent. Ask their permission to engage their children. Ask for their advice. What would be meaningful to their child or what they would like for the child to receive from you. It's a tough scenario if there are breaches in relationship to be addressed. Never loose heart; the Lord Jesus Christ is the healer. Stay focused on Him to lead you through this process of redemption. Now, that's another book.

In 2020 I don't know if I will ever become a great grandmother as many of my friends have. (no pressure on the older boys!) That would be a most incredible blessing for me. My best friend, Pam, is celebrating the pregnancy of her oldest granddaughter. Being part of her granddaughter's life over the miles, sharing pictures, and praying for her has been a great blessing to both women. You can bet that she will be on the road to meet that little great granddaughter. That's another book.

> *"Posterity will serve him; future generations will be told about the Lord. They will proclaim his righteousness to a people yet unborn."* PSALM 22: 30–31

What happens when they break your heart? If there exists a family whose grandmother has not had her heart broken, I would love to meet that family. We must always remember that volition is involved. As we have examined the role of the grandmother, it can be assumed that, because of the human condition, those whom we love the most will make decisions that disappoint and hurt us. At this moment it is important to remember that God loves our grandchildren more than we do. He desires their return to Him more than we do. Remember those open arms? Keep them open when the going gets rough. Lean with all of your might on the "Everlasting Arms." He will never fail us, and we can take great comfort in Him.

What if you don't want to be as engaged with your grandchildren as I have described? That's the choice of many. There are so many ways of "grandparenting". I celebrate you as you are writing your story.

This is mine.

Diana Severance, author, seminary professor, and curator of the Dunham Family Bible Museum at Houston Baptist University, has chronicled the lives of Christian women for 21 centuries in her book, "Her-Story: 366 Devotions for 21 Centuries of the Church." (Severance, Diana, Her-Story, Christian Focus Publications, 2016). It was a blessed exercise for me to go through the book with a look at individual women as well as the flow of history and where they fit it. Up and down, ebb and flow, the life of the individual is a powerful story. You have one. I have one. Nancy Lee DeMoss Wolgemuth, author, speaker, and radio talk host, encourages us on her radio program to be aware that our stories are designed to bring testimony to the Great God we serve and to encourage others. She also encourages us to write down our stories!

As Nana, this is mine.

Addendum #1
An Open Letter to My Grandchildren
2019

★ ★ ★

Hunter, Jackson, Joshua, Lily, Jacob, Joe, Georgia, Genny,

Nana is "writing" again, and I can hear the collective response of "oh, yay" from my grandchildren! This time I am composing an open letter to them.

Not wishing to sound like an "old person" who complains of the way things are I am actually very grieved with the way things are today. My grandchildren are growing up in a world that is wracked with evil at every turn. To call our culture by any other name is deluding ourselves and ducking from the truth.

While there is "nothing new under the sun," this is a new invasion for American thought. Evil has invaded nations since the beginning of time. The enemy never sleeps and finds his way into a culture when its guard has been relaxed. I believe we have been lulled into a false sense of security which has given way to a dangerous way of thinking. It invades our lives, our classrooms, our video games and weakens our ability to identify and stand on Truth.

The luring call to ignore God, disobey God, and rewrite His rules has seduced us. Nothing is absolute. Consequences are dissolved into bland excuses. The ability to see and answer hard questions of our day has been lost. Oh, that you will be able to think with the spiritual tools the Lord provides!!

Listen to Deuteronomy 8:10: "when you have eaten and are satisfied, you shall bless the Lord your God for the good land which He has given you. Beware lest you forget the Lore your God by not keeping His commandments and His ordinances and His statutes which I am commanding you today, lest when you have eaten and are satisfied… then your heart becomes proud, and; you forget the Lord your God who brought you out of the land of Egypt… but you shall remember the Lord your God for it is He who has given you power to make wealth that He may confirm His covenant which He swore to your fathers…."

This is a national warning. America has been blessed with prosperity from the Lord, and now our nation has turned our backs on the God Who prospered us. He has been systematically removed from our national conversation, and I foresee that it is only getting worse. Thank the Lord for the remnant of believers who will neither compromise nor shrink under the persecution. May each of you find your rock upon which to stand and your voices. May you know what you think because you have learned it from the Word of God. And may you NOT compromise His doctrine (commandments).

Know that your nation will suffer. "God is not mocked…what a man sows, that also shall he reap." Judgment will come. I am sorry that you just might be part of this time in our history when we collectively suffer the consequences. The decisions are yours, but I do pray that you are part of the solution, not part of the problem.

God does not interfere with the volition of man. Man makes his decisions and then must live by them. Individuals combine to the collective choices of a nation. In that sense, "we" are responsible. But we as individuals get to be part of the solution when we know and live by His Word.

When the soul of a person is empty, which means no information from God's Word, no verses memorized, no understanding of Scripture… then a vacuum exists. I'm sure you know people who have no firm doctrinal thinking in their souls. When that happens all manner of "mess" comes into that vacuum: thinking, depression, confusion, reaction, anger, hatred, blame, compromise, rebellion, and on and on. There is much arrogance and self-centered thinking. "I want what I want." "Me first."

The Bible calls it "every man doing what is right in his own eyes." And that is NEVER God's way. We don't get to choose what is right and what is wrong. In our nation people don't even want to say that there is an absolute standard. "Anything goes" is the mantra of the day. Well, God does not establish it that way. I pray that your standard of thinking and making decisions will be absolute standards from the Word of God. They are not mysteries that are hidden. They are there for us to learn.

What you put into your soul will be evidenced by what you think. And what you think determines what you do and the decisions you make. What you THINK is what you ARE. The one with a soul full of nothing but a vacuum will fill it with evil. That person will pick up a gun and kill or rape or destroy. So we should not be surprised with what individuals are doing in our nation. "We" will continue to implode individually and corporately. What we see is merely the implosion of a nation that has ignored God, lost its way, and is doing nothing about the problem.

God is mot mocked—nor is He surprised. He is my shield and my protection as He has been throughout history for other believers when it is dark and the lights go out.

I believe He issues us a call to arms for such a time as this. He is our security. He will protect His own according to His will.

Now comes the good part! There is great hope for you. He has put you here for such a time as this. I have shared with you, as have your wonderful parents, stories of believers who lived in difficult times and stood strong to be victorious. YOU will be champions in this day. Your older brothers/cousins are showing you how that works. I am so grateful that you are following.

This I know for sure: Your God will protect you and He will require from you obedience. My mentor taught me: God only expects two things from us—absolute obedience and complete surrender.

God IS and He ACTS. Let us always be on the right side of history so we can watch these truths unfold.

I have prayed for each one of you all of your lives. Prayer is our great weapon. Use it and use it with wisdom from His Word.

I love you dearly and am so grateful to be part of launching eight amazing people into this world… for such a time as this.

Nana

About the Author

Marsha Griffith Eckermann is a wife, mother, grandmother and "child of the Most High King." He has led her in many directions over her lifetime. She is a graduate of Houston Baptist University and has been a community volunteer in Houston, TX for most of her life. She worked in children's ministry in her church for over 25 years where she taught children and then mentored teachers in how to teach children. She now embraces the joy of passing on her love of the Word of God to her grandchildren. Having served on many boards, Marsha is founding chairman of the Komen Houston Breast Cancer Affiliate and currently serves on the A.D. Players board of directors. In 2018 was awarded "Spiritual Grandmother of the Year" by Inspire Women, a national ministry for women. Marsha is first a homemaker and has three grown children, three step children, and eight grandchildren. She and her husband,

L.D, live in Houston where they love every minute of the life the Lord has given them.

★ ★ ★

Marsha may be reached at
Mgenanacamp@att.net